WORLD BANK TECHNICAL PAPER NUMBER 163

Beyond Syndicated Loans

Sources of Credit for Developing Countries

John D. Shilling, editor

The World Bank
Washington, D.C.

Technical Papers are published to communicate the results of the Bank's work to the development community with the least possible delay. The typescript of this paper therefore has not been prepared in accordance with the procedures appropriate to formal printed texts, and the World Bank accepts no responsibility for errors.

The findings, interpretations, and conclusions expressed in this paper are entirely those of the author(s) and should not be attributed in any manner to the World Bank, to its affiliated organizations, or to members of its Board of Executive Directors or the countries they represent. The World Bank does not guarantee the accuracy of the data included in this publication and accepts no responsibility whatsoever for any consequence of their use. Any maps that accompany the text have been prepared solely for the convenience of readers; the designations and presentation of material in them do not imply the expression of any opinion whatsoever on the part of the World Bank, its affiliates, or its Board or member countries concerning the legal status of any country, territory, city, or area or of the authorities thereof or concerning the delimitation of its boundaries or its national affiliation.

The material in this publication is copyrighted. Requests for permission to reproduce portions of it should be sent to the Office of the Publisher at the address shown in the copyright notice above. The World Bank encourages dissemination of its work and will normally give permission promptly and, when the reproduction is for noncommercial purposes, without asking a fee. Permission to photocopy portions for classroom use is not required, though notification of such use having been made will be appreciated.

The complete backlist of publications from the World Bank is shown in the annual *Index of Publications*, which contains an alphabetical title list (with full ordering information) and indexes of subjects, authors, and countries and regions. The latest edition is available free of charge from the Distribution Unit, Office of the Publisher, Department F, The World Bank, 1818 H Street, N.W., Washington, D.C. 20433, U.S.A., or from Publications, The World Bank, 66, avenue d'Iéna, 75116 Paris, France.

ISSN: 0253-7494

All of the authors were part of the Financial Advisory Group at the World Bank when these papers were written. Richard Brun is a financial economist in the Europe, Middle East, and North Africa Country Department. Marcus Fedder is with the European Bank for Reconstruction and Development. Sudarshan Gooptu is a consultant to the Financial Advisory Services Group. Mohua Mukherjee is a financial economist to the Financial Advisory Services Department. Nirmaljit Singh Paul is a financial policy analyst in the Financial Policy Department. John D. Shilling is the Manager of Financial Advisory Services in the Cofinancing and Financial Advisory Services Department.

Library of Congress Cataloging-in-Publication Data

Beyond syndicated loans : sources of credit for developing countries /
    John D. Shilling, editor.
        p.   cm. — (World Bank technical paper, ISSN 0253-7494 ; no.
163)
    Includes bibliographical references.
    ISBN 0-8213-1962-0
    1. Investments, Foreign—Developing countries.   2. Loans, Foreign-
-Developing countries.   I. Shilling, John D., 1943-   .
    II. Series.
HG5993.B44   1991
336.3'435'091724—dc20   91-39294
                                                                CIP

FOREWORD

The existence of the debt crisis over the past decade made it very difficult for most developing countries to obtain voluntary external financing from private markets. Access to foreign capital flows was severely restricted for those engaged in restructuring due to their past repayment performance and doubts about their future ability to service any new debt. Even countries that honored all their scheduled payments often faced difficulties in obtaining new credit from commercial sources. Their credit standing was affected by generalized perceptions -- or mis-perceptions -- about the creditworthiness of developing countries. Although syndicated lending to developing countries has virtually ceased, other forms of external credit are available. Countries with good payment records can still access various markets, though not as easily as in the past.

The Financial Advisory Services (FAS) unit in the Cofinancing and Financial Advisory Services Department provides advice to developing countries on debt strategies, debt negotiations, and integrated approaches to external financial markets. In the course of doing this work, staff have developed close contacts with international capital markets and with lenders doing business in developing countries. Maintaining up to date information on the trends, perceptions, and instruments in these markets is a vital input into the advisory support FAS provides its clients in the World Bank and in member countries. In addition to providing this information as part of our support services, staff write papers for broader circulation on the more important of these topics.

These papers derive from such efforts. They have been circulated internally in the Bank, but they are of sufficiently broad interest to be made available to a wider audience. The three topics cover a spectrum of financing available to developing countries, including those emerging from debt crises. Together, they give a broad overview of the options available to countries and the requisites for accessing different credit markets. The papers present a good overview for those interested in the variety of instruments available in world capital markets, and they offer hope that developing countries can again access external credit after the near complete demise of voluntary syndicated lending.

John Niehuss,

Director, Cofinancing and
Financial Advisory Services

ACKNOWLEDGEMENTS

The Role and Cost of Short-Term Trade Credit

This paper has been written by Sudarshan Gooptu and Richard Brun (CFSFA). Contributions by David Fite, Atsuko Horiguchi and Bratin Sanyal are greatly appreciated. The authors would like to thank John Shilling and John Taylor for many helpful comments and suggestions.

Promoting Limited Recourse Project Finance to Developing Countries

When this paper was written Nirmaljit Singh Paul was a Financial Officer in the Cofinancing and Financial Advisory Services Department of the World Bank. He is currently a Senior Financial Policy Analyst in the Risk Management and Financial Policy Department. The findings, interpretations, and conclusions are the author's and should not be attributed to the World Bank, its Board of Directors, its management or any of its member countries.

The Reemergence of Developing Countries in the International Bond Markets

This paper was written by Marcus Fedder and Mohua Mukherjee (CFSFA). It is an extension of their earlier paper examining the successful reentry of Mexico to the international capital markets very shortly after the reduction of its commercial debt burden through a Brady deal. The authors wish to express their appreciation to John McCormick for valuable research assistance.

In addition to the assistance already recognized by the authors of each paper, I would like to express my deep appreciation to all the staff of the Financial Advisory Services unit, who have supported the authors of these papers with their commentary, general background discussions, and moral support. David Bock, who created the unit, was a guiding light for this work, and John Niehuss, our current Director, has given his full support. The painstaking task of integrating these papers and producing the finished product fell to Rose-May Colon, who has done an admirable job of it -- on top of her many other tasks. Gladys Mendez and Walter Wright assisted her in this effort. And finally, without the invaluable guidance and assistance of Connie Eysenck and Tracey Smith from Publications, none of this would have reached you, the reader. A heartfelt thanks to all.

ABSTRACT

Developing countries normally have access to a variety of foreign credits suited to different needs. As many countries have faced various difficulties in repaying their existing debt and their creditworthiness has declined, their access to these different forms of credit has become much more constrained, if not entirely blocked. Other countries with poor economic prospects may face similar difficulties, even though they do not face immediate debt crises. As countries improve their external financial situation and attempt to restore their creditworthiness, they can gain access to some forms of credit more easily than others. Careful strategies for expanding access to different markets need to be followed. These three papers examine the characteristics of different major categories of credit markets -- short term trade credit, short-to-medium term project financing, and longer term bond financing -- and how countries can establish, or reestablish, their access to them.

Trade credit is usually quite short term and often self liquidating. It is usually the last credit to be lost and the first restored. But for countries with low creditworthiness, it can be quite expensive (and hence profitable to lenders). Project financing can be tailored to cover many risks -- at a cost -- and is available for countries with promising projects. However lenders are typically only interested if there is some assurance that overall macro economic policy will allow the project to be successful commercially and if exchange risks can be covered. There is a limited range of such projects in many countries, though the possibilities grow as economies become more stable. Access to bond markets requires a much higher perception of creditworthiness, but countries that have established sound economic policies and convinced lenders of the sustainability of these policies can begin to obtain this kind of financing if they meet certain criteria.

These papers go into these methods of financing in considerable detail, describe market structures and participants, and give examples of actual lending activities. They give ranges of costs of transactions and security requirements. And they suggest strategies and actions countries can take to improve their access to these markets.

INTRODUCTION

The debt crisis of the 1980s has placed a number of burdens on the highly indebted developing countries. They have had to adjust to sharply reduced capital inflows, maintain or reschedule their service payments on existing debt, and cut domestic expenditures on current consumption and investment. This has been a painful process, and the subject of considerable dispute and debate in debtor and creditor countries alike. Substantial progress has been made in developing means of coping with the debt burden through rescheduling of official bilateral and commercial bank debt and through outright debt reduction in some cases. Debtors have made considerable progress in reforming their own economies and adapting to changed circumstances. Success on both debt relief and domestic adjustment is quite varied among countries and far from complete, but the broad outlines of what is needed and how to go about it are relatively clear. The crisis stage seems to have past, but it will be a long time before serious and widespread debt problems are behind us.

Major commercial lenders to the developing countries that encountered repayment problems have not gotten off lightly either. Many have had to shed assets and reduce staff to meet capital adequacy requirements and to stem losses. They have had to revise and often seriously curtail their business objectives and refocus their strategies. For many this has meant reducing or eliminating most their business activities in developing countries and releasing or reassigning staff with expertise in these areas. Loan Committees and Boards of Directors have been adamant about opposing new lending to developing countries with any suspicion of a debt problem. In addition, new business opportunities in Europe and other domestic markets have attracted more management attention and talent, while more recent crises in real estate and other sour investments have further sapped the banks' capacity for expansion. It is clear that for the most part, they have little appetite to return to the sovereign lending of the 1970s and early 1980s.

It has been widely accepted for a year or more that the halcyon days of jumbo syndicated loans to developing countries are over. Large scale commercial loans for essentially budget or balance of payments support are now recognized as inappropriate for both banks and borrowers. It is lamentable that this realization, so clear to many in the 1970's, arrived so late to the borrowers and lenders themselves. In fact, banks are exceedingly reluctant to engage any kind of lending to most developing countries with debt problems. This poses a severe problem to the developing countries themselves.

Taking a group of 46 highly indebted countries that the Bank uses as a reference, gross capital flows from commercial banks rose from $ 5.0 billion in 1972 to $ 31.9 billion in 1978 and a peak of $ 40.7 billion in 1982 before falling sharply to $ 22.5 billion in 1984. Gross flows have averaged only $ 4.7 billion in 1989-91. The situation with net flows (gross flows less amortization) is even more dramatic, with <u>net outflows</u> of $ 0.2 billion in the same years. Including interest payments, there has been an even larger <u>net transfer from the debtors to the creditors of $ 8.0 billion</u>! A situation which is anomalous and totally inconsistent with the medium term development requirements of these countries. Despite the debt problems on these countries, official sources have managed to sustain or increase their net flows, which averaged $ 2.4 billion in 1989-91 from bilateral sources and $ 3.9 billion from the Multilateral Development Banks to this set of countries.

It is clear that developing countries, including the severely indebted countries, are going to have to generate the vast majority of their own savings to finance their investment requirements. While this has always been true, it is all the more so now, with commercial banks reluctant to lend, and global demands for capital quite high in relations to expected savings. Domestic resources are generally most appropriate for developing countries to finance their investment. But generally, some complement of foreign resources is necessary to make best use of the domestic resources, primarily because foreign capital represents vital foreign exchange and often brings technical and marketing skills, resources in critical shortage in many of these countries. A key question is whether these developing countries can access a sufficient amount of foreign borrowing.

One continuing source of foreign exchange resources has been official lending. But this is limited, both by the capacity of the various sources of official lending -- bilateral aid programs, export credit agencies, and the multilateral lending institutions -- to expand their lending and by the fact that official lending cannot meet all the needs of developing countries for foreign resources. Official capital flows are critical for public sector investment projects, supporting adjustment programs, and providing resources for domestic financial intermediaries under certain circumstances. Official flows are not particularly well suited to support all elements of the widely applauded shift to greater emphasis on the private sector and commercial market forces as the major source of growth in developing countries. This shift will place more emphasis on expanding international trade, which will require more trade financing. Increased private sector activity will require and should attract more private source project financing. Promising activities may also allow debtors to access other financial markets beyond commercial banks -- private investors, pension funds, bond markets --especially since bonded and privately placed debt received much better treatment from debtors throughout the debt crisis.

Thus an important question facing severely indebted, and in fact many other, developing countries, is to what extent they can access private international capital markets for their very real development needs. In order to get a better understanding of the issues and possibilities for these countries to obtain resources from a variety of commercial markets, staff of the Financial Advisory Services unit of the Cofinancing and Financial Advisory Services Vice Presidency undertook several studies of sources of funding available to developing countries. This volume presents three of these studies, which cover the major sources of financing that should be available to severely indebted countries in varying degrees. The studies are not exhaustive, as it is unlikely any study could be in the fast changing world of international finance, but they give excellent background and indicate what potential exists. Some countries have already developed new forms of access, or a greatly expanded the range of possible sources of financing beyond what is described. But these countries -- Mexico, Chile, Venezuela -- are an exception and constitute the vanguard. The basic analysis remains valid.

The first paper, "The Role and Cost of Short-Term Trade Credit," by Sudarshan Gooptu and Richard Brun[1] addresses the most basic requirement for external finance -- trade credits. These are typically short term, often self liquidating, and absolutely necessary for efficient participation in world trade. Very few countries have totally lost access to trade lines, but some countries pay a high price for maintaining them. Trade credits can be structured to pose little risks for banks, but may still come at a relatively high cost to debtors, a trade-off which is discussed in the paper. Because of these features, they are typically the last forms of credit to be cut, and the first to be reestablished. Consequently,

---

[1] Presented to the Symposium on African External Finance in the 1990s, Washington, DC, September 17-18, 1990 and published in the report of the symposium. This paper is reprinted here for convenience because it completes the range of financing sources available to developing countries.

they offer the first step for a country which has lost its creditworthiness to begin to reestablish some credibility in markets. Trade credits are not only important in themselves to facilitate trade, they are also the basis for rebuilding access to medium term credit. This paper explains the the various forms of trade credits, how they are used, and the impacts of restricted access to trade credits on other economic activity. It focuses particularly on the Sub-Sahara African context, where the issue of retaining trade credits is most acute, but reference is also made to broader issues.

The second paper, "Promoting Limited Recourse Project Finance to Developing Countries," by Nirmaljit Paul addresses some promising forms of medium term project financing. As countries establish some basic level of creditworthiness, they can begin to seek out longer term financing. For most of these severely indebted countries, there is no appetite for sovereign lending, where the government is responsible for repayment. It was these same government who defaulted on the bank loans in the 1980s. But often there are attractive projects in a developing country that can attract foreign financing on the basis of the project's own potential and earnings expectation. Some foreign creditors are willing to take the "commercial" or "project" risk, but not the "country" or "transfer" risk in these projects. So they design financing packages that assure their returns are payable in foreign exchange. There deals are attractive to investment bankers, who are paid a fee for putting the deal together and who take little if any capital risk. They also offer needed capital and often foreign expertise to developing countries. Project financing offers debtors countries access to more financing and a way of establishing a better credit standing by maintaining impeccable payment records on these projects. Often it is the private sector which maintains the payment, but that also improves the reputation of the country and establishes that the government is undertaking sound policies that allow the private sector to prosper. This market is in constant evolution and the paper offers valuable insights into the structure and motivations of these operations.

The third paper, "The Reemergence of Developing Countries in the International Bond Markets," by Marcus J. J. Fedder and Mohua Mukherjee addresses a range of financing opportunities that open up as countries further enhance their creditworthiness and tap a wider range of investors. The bond markets offer both a larger variety of instruments for longer term financing and a deeper pool of funds. But access to this market is much more restrictive, and investors demand a high level of security. The paper describes the different national and cross border markets that together constitute the international capital market. (We are still a long way from a truly unified global market.) It profiles investor preferences in major markets and the principal characteristics of the instruments. Individual experiences of countries that have gained access to portions of this market are also presented as examples These demonstrate that it is possible for countries that have suffered severe debt problems to work their way back to credibility. This is an important statement, as it does confirm that successful adjustment programs can have positive results in paving the way to renewed market access on truly "voluntary" or "spontaneous" terms.

All three of these papers offer practical suggestions about how countries can improve their access to these various forms of credit. These are indicative and do not constitute formal advice, which can only be given after careful review of a country's institutions and objectives. They do provide a valuable overview of what will become the dominant forms of debt financing for developing countries in the coming years. In many regards, these forms of financing are more relevant and useful for the borrowers than the syndicated credits of the 1970s. They are directly linked to productive activities and have readily identified income streams that can be linked to repayment. This is clearly important for the lender, but also for the borrower, who is more likely to be assured that the funds being borrowed are put to productive use. What is most encouraging is that in the few months since the research was completed for these papers, the markets have become more open to a growing number of developing countries that have experienced debt problems and are working their way out of them. A surprising amount of private capital is again flowing into a number of Latin American countries. This seems to include both returning flight capital and new funds from other investors. Evidence is still very partial and anecdotal, but it is accumulating. Staff in CFS continue to monitor these developments and additional studies will be completed in the future.

John D. Shilling

CONTENTS

The Role and Cost of Short-Term Trade Credit

Sudarshan Gooptu
Richard Brun

CONTENTS

INTRODUCTION

Since the advent of the debt crisis countless studies have been conducted on public and publicly guaranteed long-term external debt of LDCs from both official and commercial creditors. These types of indebtedness of LDCs are now well defined and have been extensively analyzed. However, when it comes to short-term debt and specifically to short-term trade finance from commercial banks it is very difficult to get a clear view of the situation. Depending on the origin of statistics (e.g. BIS, IMF, OECD or World Bank) there may be discrepancies of as much as 100 percent between estimates of short-term indebtedness for the same country. These discrepancies occur due to differences in the definition and coverage used in reporting trade financing statistics.

There are several ways in which a country can acquire trade financing from abroad. These include short-term bank credit, medium-term trade credit, short-term suppliers credit, short-term financial credit and inter-bank lines, among others. The reality of short-term trade finance is extremely complicated because of the multiplicity of techniques of acquiring trade finance, particularly in the case of LDCs, where imports and exports can be financed through facilities offered by governments, multilateral organizations, commercial banks and even non-bank entities (such as multinational corporations, and trading companies).

In this study we had to make a choice on which technique to focus on. As the main purpose of the study is to analyze the possibilities for LDCs to get trade financing essential for their external trade, we decided to focus on non-guaranteed short-term trade financing. These credits can be defined as: *Credits extended by commercial banks to entities in the developing countries with an original maturity of one year or less* We assume that "commercial banks" are institutions involved in traditional banking activities. We must, nevertheless, point out that for some very sophisticated techniques (such as countertrade, forfaiting,...) investment banks can be involved, but these techniques remain relatively marginal. Only those short term trade credits which are not guaranteed by either the borrower's government or any external agency (such as Exim banks) of the creditor governments were included in the analysis. All other credits, namely bilateral, multilateral, medium and long-term public and publicly guaranteed are excluded. The knowledge of commercial short-term trade financing is very important in order to get a complete understanding of private financial flows to LDCs. This is particularly true for the very low-income countries.

Since the beginning of the debt crisis, most of the less-developed countries (especially the low-income countries) have relied on official creditors to meet their medium and long-term financing needs, since commercial banks were reducing their exposure in these countries and diverting their resources to the industrialized countries. However, the situation has been quite different for short-term financing. Short-term trade financing from official sources (e.g. Export credit agencies) has not been enough to fulfill the needs of these LDCs due to the limited resources. In addition, the financing available from these agencies is often tied to exports of the donor country and is not as flexible in its use as is warranted by the needs of the borrower.

The composition of trade in LDCs makes the need for short-term trade finance particularly acute. Specifically, these countries are mainly primary goods exporters and consumer goods importers. Producers of primary goods exports require short-term trade finance during the short production cycle involved in the production of most of these goods. Given the level and type of international trade of LDCs, it becomes imperative for them to maintain important commercial ties with commercial banks in order to get the financing necessary for these operations. Therefore, access to short- term trade lines is crucial to LDCs today and will become increasingly important as international trade continues to flourish.

It should be noted that short-term trade financing is only one of the several different types of loans (such as, medium and long-term project financing, interbank lines and overdrafts) that commercial banks provide to LDCs. One would expect the behavior of short-term lending to be influenced, to some extent, by trends in other types of bank lending operations. However, between 1982 and 1986, when banks were reducing their medium and long-term lending to LDCs, short term lending did not decrease proportionately. It just became costlier for LDCs to obtain. In most cases, countries continued to service their short-term obligations even in the face of payments difficulties on their medium and long term debt. This made short-term lending profitable for the banks.

When the rescheduling of short term obligations was permitted by the banks in the context of a more comprehensive debt restructuring agreement, new short term credits still continued to be available to the LDCs as long as they were serviced. But they were costlier to obtain. When a country went into arrears (as in the case of Peru), short term trade credits became even costlier and more difficult to obtain.

The current status of external indebtedness of certain developing countries has led to a strategy that included debt reduction (of both bilateral and commercial debt) as a way to help resolve their debt problems. Debt reduction is viewed as a way of alleviating the debt overhang of the debt-distressed less-developed countries in order to facilitate the resumption of economic growth and reopen access to international financial markets. The question that one frequently encounters in this context is whether a country will continue to receive short-term trade lines after it proceeds with a commercial debt-reduction operation. In an endeavor to find a plausible answer to this question, the determinants of short-term trade financing from commercial banks to less-developed countries (LDCs) are examined in this study.

Indeed, the answer to the above question is by no means clear. There are a wide range of instruments to support trade credits, not all of which are directly used by commercial banks, and there are many ways to increase the cost of such credits for risky clients. Due to the multiplicity of factors that influence the behavior of short-term trade lines from commercial banks (such as fees, interest rates, penalty structure, currency denomination, exchange rate movements, among others), the consequences of a debt reduction operation by one country may be quite different from those experienced by another. For example, trade lines continued to be available to Bolivia after its buyback operations. In fact, the terms on which this financing is available have improved. In the case of Brazil, short-term trade financing from commercial banks became more costly and difficult to obtain after its declaration of a moratorium on debt service payments to commercial creditors. However, short-term trade lines were quickly restored after the announcement of the interim financing agreement with commercial banks at the end of 1987.

The amount and cost of short-term trade lines from commercial banks are determined on a case-by-case basis. Our investigation has revealed that these transactions may be complex and that it may be difficult to distinguish between purely short-term trade credits and interbank lines. While it is unlikely that commercial banks would completely sever their relationships with confrontational debtors, they can make life difficult for them.

The objective of this study is to improve our understanding of the mechanics of short-term trade financing to developing countries and use all available information to deduce, in general terms, the factors that seem to be common across countries in determining the amount of short-term trade financing that is available to them at any point in time.

The first stage of this study gathered as much "market" information as possible on the factors that have been taken into consideration by commercial banks, investment houses, and trading companies when providing short-term trade lines to private importers in less- developed countries. This was achieved through interviews with key officials who are involved in this activity in the U.S. and in Europe. This exercise was quite cumbersome since the institutions which provide commercial short-term trade lines, being private entities, are not required to disclose such information to any multilateral agency. All the information obtained by us was purely voluntary. In addition, short-term trade lines are designed on a case-by-case basis. Hence, a country with severe liquidity problems at a certain point in time may be forced to accept usurious terms on short-term trade lines from one institution although loans with better terms would have been available to it at the same or a later date from some other institution. This is particularly true for those low-income countries which already have very limited access to medium and long-term financing from commercial creditors.

The general overview of trade financing activities that was gleaned from the market is provided in Section 1 of this paper. Section 2 focuses on the specific question of trade financing in Sub-Saharan African. Section 3 presents the results of the econometric analysis on the level of trade lines paper. The cross-sectional econometric study was done on thirty-two debt-distressed countries. Section 4 provides the basic conclusions of the study and provides recommendations for possible improvement in the cost of trade lines and their access to the less developed countries. Annexes I and II provide details on the data used in the quantitative analysis on the level of short term trade financing from banks to the LDCS. The terms under which trade credits were restructured in the past in selected countries are shown in Annex III of the paper.

1. MAIN FEATURES OF TRADE FINANCING

A.   Status of Statistical Information on Trade Lines

The nature of trade financing from commercial banks to developing countries, which is both rapidly changing and is comprised of numerous financial instruments, makes accurate measurement difficult. Moreover, there is a fine line which differentiates trade finance from other categories of short term debt, especially inter-bank lines. However, there exist several sources for measuring at least some elements of the flow of trade finance. Each source has its limitations but it is possible to determine some basic data which may provide a base for any quantitative study of the various aspects of trade financing.

Some data on short term debt is available from the standard sources for medium and long term public and publicly-guaranteed debt such as the BIS, OECD and DRS reporting agencies. However, short-term debt data presented in each of these sources is not necessarily only short-term trade financing from commercial banks. Other forms include certain balance of payments measures such as bridge loans, accumulated arrears and cross- border bank liabilities. The accuracy of any reporting system is strained by the rapidly changing nature of trade lines which may have terms shorter than the normal reporting intervals. Listed below are the main sources identified and some additional factors which must be considered when using any of these sources for an analysis of the availability short term trade finance:

World Bank: World debt tables
Short term debt data is provided by debtor government. Short term debt data is analyzed for accuracy to the extent possible by World Bank staff. However, given the difficulty in verifying any of these figures and the fact that no effort is made to specifically identify trade lines, the DRS data cannot be considered a reliable basis for an analysis of the extent of short-term trade finance.

BIS: Semi-annual report on external indebtedness
The semi-annual report on external indebtedness provides a breakdown of loans by maturity. It also provides a breakdown by debtor (Central banks, Inter-bank lines, Clients). Trade lines are not specifically identified. In addition, the coverage of the banks in the BIS semi-annual reports is smaller than that in its quarterly report. BIS covers only banks from declaring countries (mainly OECD countries), loans from other countries are not covered. Until recently, the BIS reported maturity at remaining time till full repayment of all loans rather than the original maturity of the loans. Hence, short term loans included medium and long term loans that would attain full maturity during the calender year in question.

OECD: Financing and External Debt of Developing   countries
This data base is recorded in the AREMOS data base of the IMF on a semi-annual basis. The export credits data are disintegrated into suppliers' and financial credits. Export credit data provided by the IMF (AREMOS) database may differ from the OECD's published figures on export credits because the OECD data contain arrears from long-term trade related credits in addition to the reported short-term export credits data (which is recorded in the IMF database).

OECD-BIS: External Debt Statistics
This annual publication provides a breakdown of trade related credits extended by banks and non-banks entities. However, a further breakdown of short-term trade finance from banks is not available. This makes it difficult to distinguish between short term trade lines and other short-term financing such as

inter-bank lines. Nevertheless, this is one of the few consistent and complete sources of available data on short term financing from commercial banks.

It is possible to find a reasonable estimate of short-term trade lines on a country-by-country basis by cross-checking the statistical data from these sources. BIS and OECD-BIS statistics seem to be the most appropriate for this purpose. Since data on short-term credits are available along with data on inter-bank lines, it is possible to get a rough estimate of short term trade lines by subtraction. Comparing this data with figures on the composition of foreign trade on a country-by-country basis might offer a satisfactorily close estimate of the reality of short term trade financing from commercial banks.

B.   Overview of Financial Instruments for Trade Financing

When goods are traded between two parties, it is necessary to devise mechanisms that will be used to complete the related financial transaction. This is particularly true for international trade due to the complexity and riskiness of the exchange. Trade finance has been one of the oldest financial techniques used in history. Some of the basic principles used in devising innovative trade financing instruments are discussed in this section of the paper. In this study we will concentrate on the instruments of widespread use for trade financing to LDCs (a complete description is beyond the scope of his study).

Any trade has two areas related to the settlement of the transaction, namely, the exchange process, or the actual transferring of payment and ownership of the goods, and the risk associated with the transaction, i.e the risk of delayed, or, non-payment by the buyer and the risk of non delivery by the seller. Trade financing instruments can be understood as ways to divide these two areas among the numerous parties potentially involved. The parties involved will depend on the specifics of each transaction and can include the buyer, the seller, commercial banks, third party trading or financial intermediaries, as well as, governmental agencies.

The process of payment and the transfer of ownership of the goods can occur in a number of ways. At one end of the spectrum,- for countries with sound economic situations - goods can be sent on account with ownership being transferred immediately to the buyer and the payment due immediately or after a short period of time. On the other end of the spectrum, the supplier requires cash or payment in advance for the goods. In between the two extremes are a series of financial instruments and structures to regulate the flow of payments and ownership. One of the most important determinants of the payment method to be utilized in any particular transaction is the level of risk in the transaction. The seller must weigh the risk and the amount of protection desired against becoming non-competitive for the buyer. The principal risks involved in international trade are summarized below:

Commercial Credit Risk: This type of risk can be split into two categories;
    Acceptance risk in which the buyer does not accept the shipment, and
    Financial risk which is the risk of slow payment or financial insolvency.

Political Risks: These risks are tied to the sovereign action of a foreign government that can prevent payment because of lack of foreign currency. It also deals with political disturbances that can prevent the shipment from being accepted by the buyer/importer.

Documentary Risk: This risk deals with problems tied to the compliance of the documentation with regulations in the importing countries. Failure to comply with regulations could lead to delays in clearing goods through customs and in some cases to confiscation of goods.

Interest Rate Risk: When financing terms are fixed, changes in the interest rate can become unfavorable for the seller or the buyer.

Foreign Exchange Risk: Often, exports and imports are paid in a currency other than that of the country (this is almost always the case in LDCs), a change in the value of the domestic currency during the trade process can result in a severe loss for the importer or the exporter.

Instruments of Trade Financing
Relationship between Cost and Risk

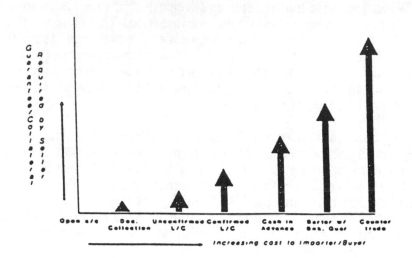

To face all these risks exporters and importers will choose appropriate techniques which are briefly described below. Chart 1.1 summarizes the different types of techniques used depending on the situation of the buyer and the seller in such commercial operations.

1. Documentary Collection and Letters of Credit

The easiest and cheapest way to finance trading is the <u>Clean Collection</u> (or Open account transaction) where a buyer sends a purchase order and the payment instrument (Bill of exchange, promissory note or check) without any other trade documents to the seller and without any explicit intervention of a commercial bank.

Costs: For such a transaction, the costs are minimum since no intermediary is involved. It will include such items as telexes, phone calls and international drafts. In practice, for a simple operation, the cost can be as low as US$20 to US$30.

Who bears the risk: This technique is generally considered to be the most favorable for a buyer of a good. In fact, by accepting this technique the seller bears all risks related to a international trade transaction and has few measures of recourse in case of problems.

This technique is generally used during common trading activities between the majority of companies of good standing in the OECD countries. For example, exporters in the U.S relied on this technique for 65% of their business with EEC importers in 1989. But in most

LDCs only companies with good international standing (subsidiaries of multinational corporations or large local conglomerates) have access to this technique for their foreign business. The diagram below shows the principle of the technique.

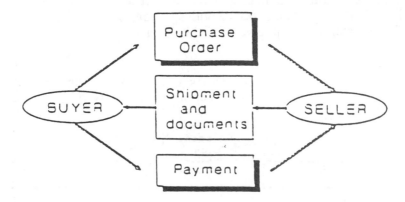

Instruments for Trade Financing
Open Account

Documentary Collection

      Documentary Collection is very similar to the technique of "clean collection" (Open Account). The difference being that in Documentary Collection commercial or transport documents are included for completing the transaction. Typically, documents give full or partial title of the goods to the holder of the documents. In fact, "Documentary collection" is a mechanism that allows the seller to retain ownership of the goods until payment is received or is almost certainly going to be received. With a documentary collection (also known as a "bill of exchange"), a bank acts as the agent of the seller and holds the title document of the goods until the buyer either pays - i.e. "documents against payment" - or accepts the obligation to pay - i.e. "document against acceptance". Under a documentary collection scheme the bank has control of the documents although it does not bear any risk, except the risk of mishandling the documents. The banking system only plays an intermediary role that does not extend to providing guarantees for the documents or enforcement of responsibilities on either the buyer or seller's part under the sale contract.

Costs: As in the case of open account, documentary collection can be considered as an inexpensive mechanism for conducting trade. In fact, the costs are limited to communication costs (phone, telex) and some fees for the bank involved. Generally, the effective cost of doing a documentary collection is under US$100.

Who bears the risks: Since the documents of title to the goods being traded are held by a bank during a transaction, the seller has a greater degree of security than with an open account. The seller can specify to his banker that the buyer will not get title until he has paid cash or the bank has accepted a check drawn on the buyer. The buyer can inspect the documents before payment or acceptance and as long as the documents are satisfactory, he partially satisfies his objective of getting assurance on the quality and quantity of the goods in question. The seller still bears all the different risks inherent in an international transaction, namely:

> Acceptance of the goods by the buyer
> Credit risk of the buyer
> Political risk of the buyer's country
> Foreign exchange convertibility risk
> Failure to claim custom risk

For all these reasons documentary collection has almost the same status for exporters as clean collection. It is mainly used for international commercial transactions in the OECD countries. This technique is not of widespread use in LDCs, if used at all, it is reserved for companies with high standing in the view of the seller.

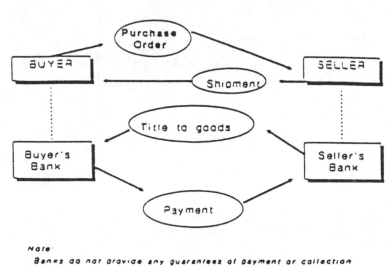

Instruments of Trade Financing
Documentary Collection

Note:
Banks do not provide any guarantees of payment or collection

A Letter of Credit is the other basic building block of international trade. The standard, or documentary letter of credit, is a means whereby the bank not only controls the documents, but also accepts some of the risks of the transaction. The risks which the bank may take are:

> Credit risk of the buyer
> Political risks of the buyer's country
> Foreign exchange convertibility risk

A letter of credit is a written undertaking by a bank. (i.e., the "issuing bank") to the seller (i.e., the "beneficiary") in accordance with the instructions of the buyer (i.e., the "applicant") to effect payment up to a determined amount within a prescribed time period against prescribed documents, provided these are correct and in order. The documents encompass those needed for the commercial purpose of effecting the sale, insurance and transport (usually bills of lading). Payment is made either against presentation of the documents on their own, or against the documents together with a bill (known as a draft) drawn against the bank where the letter of credit is available. The draft may be a sight draft, or a time draft payable a specified number of days after a specific date, commonly the bill of lading date. Two banks are generally involved in a letter of credit: The "issuing" bank which is the buyer's bank and the "advising" bank which is a bank in the seller's country and is usually the seller's bank. The advising bank undertakes transmission of the credit and authenticates the validity of the issuing bank's execution but undertakes no commitment to pay the seller.

The letter of credit (L/C) is a very adaptable instrument that can fit any situation. Three main types of L/Cs exist:

(a) The Revocable L/C is a very interesting instrument for the buyer since it can be amended or cancelled without prior notice until the moment of payment.

Costs: For a three-month letter, some importers have to pay 0.9% per quarter on the value of the letter. Some banks charge a minimum of US$500 for any unconfirmed L/C whatever the value of the letter. Between US$30 and US$40 must be added for wire, telephone and telex costs.

Who bears the risk: In this case the seller bears all the risks, particularly when the goods have been shipped. In fact this instrument provides the suppliers with no greater security than a documentary collection or an order to pay.

(b) The Irrevocable L/C cannot be amended or cancelled without the agreement of all parties involved. This instrument offers less adaptability for the buyer and a better guaranteed of payment to the seller. This form of L/C results from an agreement between the two parties and is relatively equitable for both. This partly explains why it is the most widely used technique of trade financing.

Costs: They are the same those for a revocable L/C.

Who bears the risks: As explained above, risks are shared between buyer and seller. In this case, where the letter of credit is unconfirmed, the seller accepts more risk than the buyer. Nevertheless, this instrument offers a relatively good protection to the seller for conducting normal business trading in a country with a relatively sound economy.

(c) The Confirmed Irrevocable Letter of Credit is a L/C confirmed by the advising bank. This instrument offers the maximum guarantee of payment to the seller since there is a pledge from the seller's bank and a pledge from a bank in the buyer's country. This technique is most often used for conducting business in a country whose economic situation is not so sound, particularly LDCs.

Costs: For a three-month letter, some importers have to pay 1.3% per quarter on the value of the letter. Some banks charge a minimum of US$700 whatever the value of the letter. In addition, costs for wire, telephone and telex between US$30 and US$40 are added.

Who bears the risks: Clearly, among "classical" short-term trade financing techniques, the CILC provides the seller with the best guarantees. This explains why it is often used in LDCs with macroeconomic problems. For the buyer (in the LDC), this adds new requirements and is costly. In addition, the buyer often has no room to negotiate and must accept the conditions of the seller. In a typical operation, most sellers (exporters) in OECD countries do not accept confirmations from the LDC importers' domestic banks in the case of most LDCs. Hence, a foreign bank with offices in the buying country has to issue a L/C which is, in turn, confirmed by the OECD seller's bank.

In this way, the seller's bank bears some of the political and foreign currency convertibility risks associated with the transaction.

Most trade finance transactions utilize documentary collections and L/Cs as their basis and are adapted to the specific commercial transaction. L/Cs can be tailored for different purposes, some of them allow banks to increase their liquidity (Bankers acceptances), others serve the interests of middlemen (Back to Backs), others are useful when there are a series of repetitive shipments (Revolving credits).

Banker's Acceptances (B/As) are the most common derivative trade finance product. A Banker's acceptance is created when a commercial bank sells one or two types of obligations on the secondary market: A confirmed letter of credit or an obligation which is based on the direct borrowing of the buyer or seller. The amount a purchaser who has recourse to the commercial bank pays for the BA is the face amount less some discount. There is an important market for BAs in developed countries, however, only a few LDCs currently have access to this market.

Back-to-Backs are specially designed for commercial transactions involving middlemen, which is often the case in LDCs. A Back-to-back can be issued to allow the middleman to assign the proceeds of one letter of credit to a second letter of credit which pays the suppliers. Banks are generally reluctant to open Back-to-back credits without special security. Generally, banks confine the issue of back-to-backs to situations where there is an alternative source of repayment. In the case of LDCs which are in a precarious economic situation a collateral can be required from the buyer.

Revolving credit schemes are devised when trade flows are repetitive. These schemes are implemented in order to avoid the need to issue new letters of credit each time there is a transaction. There are two categories of revolving credit: (i) credit revolving in time. For example, there may be a credit of US$15,000 revolving each month during one year. In this case, the credit of US$15,000 is available each month even if it has not been drawn the previous month (available credit can be added from one month to other), and (ii) credit revolving in value. In this case a credit of US$15,000 is renewed when it is completely drawn. Revolving letters of credit arrangements are structured to renew either automatically or by amendments which allows the issuing bank to check the credit of its customer before agreeing to each transaction.

2. Barter and Countertrade

Barter and countertrade are techniques of growing importance for trading with LDCs, but are much less developed than L/Cs. The OECD has estimated that these techniques accounted for around 10% of the world trade in 1985. They accounted for 15% percent of the East-West trade and around 6-8% of the North-South trade. As the economic and financial situation of most LDCs worsened during the last ten years, many of them, particularly the poorest, have had to increase their reliance on these techniques of financing in order to maintain the minimum level of imports necessary to their development. Some of them have been forced by private creditors to accept those techniques even though they were extremely costly to the buyers/importers. The techniques utilized are diverse and, generally speaking, are tailored to the requirements of the countries and the specific transaction.

Barter

Pure barter is the exchange of goods for goods without the use of any monetary instrument. This pure form of barter does not exist any more. Today a monetary standard is used in any barter agreement, at least to appraise the value of goods exchanged. Since simultaneity of exchange is not always possible, this situation implies the need for guarantees. For most of low income indebted countries even barter trade as accompanied by several risks such as: the risk of quality of goods, pricing, risk of non- delivery. For these reasons several techniques have been developed to match these risks.

Previous Invoice of Goods is often required by OECD counterparts to be certain of getting the quality of goods agreed in the contract. In this case, it is the seller to the LDC who asks for a banking guarantee. This guarantee covers the risk of non delivery by the OECD exporter. The amount of guarantee is reduced as the goods are delivered against presentation of documents.

Barter by L/C is a technique by which two L/Cs are exchanged between importer and exporter. The L/C issued in favor of the OECD exporter by a foreign bank will be supplied by funds coming from the sale of the products given in the barter. The bank of the OECD exporter will not transfer the currencies tied to the L/C in favor of the foreign client, unless it receives the shipping documents prior to the agreed upon deadline. This technique offers flexibility to the barter contract and offers greater security to the OECD exporter.

Escrow Account: This account is governed by a covenant between the exporter in an OECD country and his client in a LDC. It is managed by a "neutral" bank, credited with the proceeds of the sale of the goods from the LDC and debited with the payments due to the exporter from the OECD. This account can offer an excellent security and is often used for such transactions. The safety of an escrow account depends on the quality of agreements between the two parties. The escrow account offers great flexibility for external trade involving LDCs in troubled financial situations. Through this technique it is possible to bring together numerous small exporters from OECD countries who could debit the escrow account after each operation.

The diagram below shows the principle of this technique (with banking guarantee):

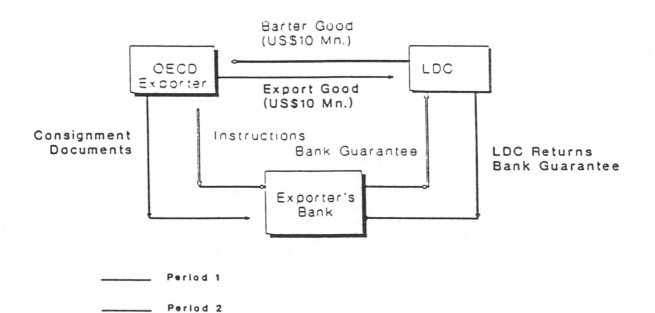

Instruments of Trade Financing
Barter with Commercial Bank Guarantee

Countertrade

Theoretically, countertrade is very similar to barter. The main difference is that a part of the transaction is done with cash. In this technique, exports and imports are included in the same contract. The interdependence of the two operations can be considered as the main limitation of this type of technique. Litigation on the buying side of the contract reflects upon the selling. Risk in a countertrade operation is the same as in the case of barter, particularly for the delivery of the goods after the export from OECD country (quality of goods, price,..). For trading with countries having economic difficulties, the delivery of the goods is often required before any goods are exported from the OECD country. In any contract of countertrade a rate of compensation (the part paid in cash) depending on the bargaining power of the two parties, and the goods exported

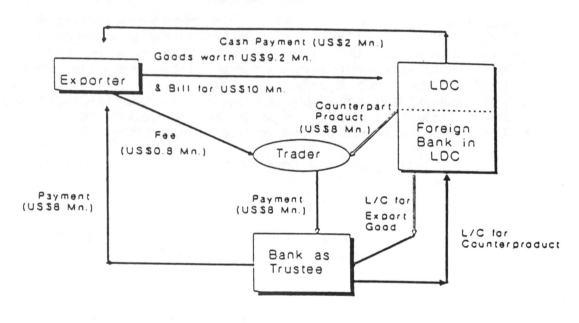

Instruments of Trade Financing
Countertrade

Forfaiting

Forfaiting is a technique primarily created to improve liquidity of operations arising from deliveries of goods and services. Since it implies the existence of a secondary market, this technique can be very useful for LDCs. It offers more safety to the counterparts in commercial transactions and provides a good market value for their country risk. Forfeiting consists of discounting without recourse trade or other receivables owned by an exporter and remitting to him, in a lump sum, the proceeds of the discount. Depending on the nature of the goods, the credit is offered for a period from six months up to seven years; it is evidenced by trade bills (Bills of exchange or promissory notes) or alternatively, by book receivables. The receivables are usually guaranteed by a bank.

In this transaction, the forfaiter (i.e. the buyer of the trade bills) waives its rights to a recourse to the seller and to any prior holder in case of default. In this way, the exporter has completely eliminated its export finance related risk which is now taken on by the market. These include:

Commercial risk

Political risk

Non-transfer risk, and

Currency risk if billing in foreign currency.

As opposed to other export financing techniques, bills negotiated in forfaiting operations are generally freely transferable. This gives bankers the possibility of selling the bills on the secondary market which is chiefly located in Europe and consists of banks, specialized institutions and investors. The liquidity and competition on the secondary market obviously have a favorable impact on the terms granted by the forfaiter to the exporter on the primary market. Discounting without recourse is increasingly used in the transfer of trade and financial bills.

2. TRADE FINANCING IN SUB-SAHARAN AFRICA

A. General Overview of Trade Financing in Sub-Saharan Africa

If we observe the situation of Sub-Saharan Africa regarding commercial bank financing, we can notice quite an atypical situation compared to other LDCs. Most of the low-income countries of Sub-Saharan Africa have relied on official creditors to meet their medium and long-term financing needs, since commercial banks were dramatically reducing their exposure in these countries and diverting their resources to the industrialized countries after the 1982 crisis. Short term trade financing from official sources (e.g. Export credit agencies) was also reduced and has not been enough to fulfill the needs of these LDCs. Therefore these countries relied proportionally more on private short term financing than on medium term financing. This seems particularly true if we compare some estimates of the part of short term trade financing on total commercial debt in middle income countries (mainly in Latin America) and in low income African countries. On 10 African countries in which we have reliable estimates, short term lines represent around 34% of the medium and long term debt. In Latin America short term lines represent only 5.7%. The table below shows the figures on a country by country basis. These figures must be

TABLE 1: Share of Short term Trade lines in Total Commercial Debt: Selected Countries.

(as of end–1988)

Country	Total Comm. Debt (US$ Mn.)	o/w. ST Trade Finance 1/ (US$ Mn.)	Percent
AFRICA			
Burundi	20	20	100.0%
Congo	310	125	40.3%
Guinea	30	15	50.0%
Madagascar	110	24	21.8%
Mozambique	279	23	8.2%
Niger	105	55	52.4%
Senegal	80	55	68.8%
Tanzania	140	20	14.3%
Togo	49	21	42.9%
Zaire	441	150	34.0%
Subtotal	1,564	508	32.5%
LATIN AMERICA			
Argentina	30,400	1,000	3.3%
Brazil	67,600	3,300	4.9%
Chile	11,000	2,100	19.1%
Venezuela	26,600	2,900	10.9%
Mexico	63,400	4,200	6.6%
Subtotal	199,000	13,500	6.8%
Total	200,564	14,008	7.0%

SOURCE: World Bank "World Debt Tables", 1989-90 except those indicated by an '·'. For those countries, the data has been obtained more recently by the Governments of the countries concerned.

1/ World Bank Staff estimates.

cautiously analyzed because they partly reflect the fact that the access of poorer countries to medium and long term financing is limited. They also point out the fact that these countries rely more than others on short term financing.

In fact, Sub Saharan African countries are more fragile than others regarding the financing of their trade. On one hand, the structure of their external trade implies probably more short term trade finance, and on the other, their institutional structure is less adapted than in other countries to manage these techniques.

1.   External Trade in Sub-Saharan African Countries

In Sub-Saharan Africa, exports are heavily concentrated on few products. In 1987 figures showed that in low income countries the share of commodities and primary products on total exports reached 92% of total exports (if we included petroleum the share was 99%). Short term financing from commercial banks is particularly required to finance these exports as the specific production cycle involved in the production of most of these goods involves it.

Imports are mainly composed of commodities (oil, food)and consumer goods. In 1987, in low income Sub-Saharan African countries the share of these goods averaged 66%. As these goods need more short term financing than others (capital goods can be financed on medium term, often official, project basis), this situation increases the need for these financing, compared with other countries.

The particular structure of imports also increases the cost of financing. The average value of import contracts signed by most African countries is generally low. For example, in three IDA-only countries around 60% of all contracts are under US$10,000. Since there is a minimum cost charged by banks (US$500 on letters of credit) the relative cost (5% or more) is much higher than in other countries.

2.   The Question of Banking Systems in Sub-Saharan Africa

Obtaining trade lines for an importer implies the existence of a good banking system with adequate technical know-how and good relations with the international banking community. In most African countries, a limited banking system and the lack of know-how limit the access to trade financing. In fact, trade financing is mainly arranged through subsidiaries of multinational banks operating in the African country concerned.

Financing is even more critical for exports. To work efficiently, exporters need a good banking system as well as trading companies and some kind of a guarantee mechanism. This institutional environment is rudimentary or even nonexistent in African countries. On the pure financing environment, there are no money markets or government rediscount facilities to convert financial paper into liquidity. These facilities do exist in the highly indebted middle income countries (Brazil, Mexico) but not in Sub Saharan Africa. Therefore, these countries rely entirely on foreign international banks for the financing of their exports.

B . Consequences of the Economic Crisis on the Practice of Trade Financing in Sub-Saharan Africa

Since the beginning of the debt crisis in the early 1980s the reality of trade finance in LDCs has become increasingly complex. Before that period, trade financing was one of the most traditional activities of the banking business, and it was considered as the most secure among loans extended to countries. At that time it was very easy for a banker to adopt a gradual response to the worsening economic situation in a determined country. Since the credits were short term in nature, a banker could easily cut a line or increase the cost of it when a country faced economic or financial problems. The debt crisis opened a new era in this activity. At the end of the seventies, several LDCs facing external deficits increased their short term indebtedness - inter-bank lines and trade lines - dramatically to finance part of their balance of payments gap. When the crisis broke out, banks having trade or inter-bank lines with LDCs were trapped. In effect, short term lines became long term credit, and between 1982 and 1985 almost all trade lines to the major LDCs were rescheduled or extended, and in some cases were included in the base for the calculation of concerted new money requirements for the countries. Since then, bankers have become much more reluctant than in the past to open new lines to LDCs. This new attitude was particularly true in Sub Saharan Africa. The financing conditions for trade credit in rescheduling agreements that were negotiated between 1983 and 1988 are provided in Annex 3.

1. The Curtailment of Classical Trade Financing

(a) The economic factor

The type of instrument used for financing the trade of a country is closely related to its status and its economic situation. In practice, the richer the country and the sounder its economic situation, the simpler and cheaper the techniques of trade applied to that country. In the case of Sub-Saharan Africa the worsening economic situation has led to a dramatic decrease of Letters of Credit for exporters from OECD. In the case of U.S exporters, "world guide for exporters", a widely circulated professional publication, showed in the first quarter of 1989 that no more L/C was available for Africa. The table below shows the data gathered from this publication:

TABLE 2: Main Trade Financing Techniques Used for Exports Outside The United States

(In percent)

Region to which Exported	Open Account	Sight Draft	Time Draft	Unconfirmed L/C	Confirmed L/C
EEC	65	16	18	0.	1
Other Europe	51	11	9	6	22
Latin America	3	9	11	1	77
Africa	0	None	None	None	None
Middle East	6	10	15	0	69
LDCs Asia	10	15	12	14	49

Source: "The World Guide for Exporters", GBC Inc. Publication, First Quarter of 1989.

In OECD countries, exporters rely on international publications giving the rating of LDCs and the techniques recommended for any business with these countries. For instance, The Export Credits Clearing House in London regularly publishes a survey on commercial conditions in 114 countries (85 LDCs and 29 Eastern and Arab countries). A brief overview of this survey at the end of 1988 shows that:

> In 34 IDA-only countries mentioned, it is recommended to exporters to work on the basis of irrevocable letters of credit (ILC) for 9 countries, and on the basis of confirmed irrevocable letters of credit (CILC) for 19 countries. Trade is recommended without limitation on techniques in only 6 countries. None of which are in Sub-Saharan Africa.

> In the 51 other LDCs mentioned, ILC are recommended for 14 countries and CILC are recommended for only 9 countries.

When a CILC is recommended by a rating company for some country, it generally implies an unfavorable economic situation because it represents the worst classification. A recommendation of using CILC does not necessarily imply that it will, in fact, be available for that country. Although, in theory, a confirmation of credit can be obtained from a bank in the country of the importer, in practice few banks in the OECD will accept such a confirmation. They will request confirmation from another OECD bank. This explains why some countries cannot rely on these technique and must rely on other techniques to import goods from developed countries. Today, most Sub-Saharan African countries are in this situation.

The confirmation of L/Cs depends on numerous factors difficult to formalize. Even if an economic situation is very difficult some determined importers from this country can obtain confirmations because of their reputation or their financial situation. Another factor can be the nature of the product imported. The statistical survey on exports from the US to LDCs, shows that some countries can obtain CILC for certain products they import, e.g, it is easier to get a CILC for pharmaceutical goods than for a sports car.

The last factor to take into account is the international strategy of banks. US banks maintain important commercial relations with Latin America and are generally prepared to confirm L/Cs, but they have very little trade finance with Africa on the basis of letter of credit (this is confirmed on the table above). On the other hand, European banks - mainly French and British are more flexible in confirming L/Cs in Africa. But some countries cannot obtain any confirmation from any bank in the OECD. These were the ones that first suffered a dramatic reduction in their imports to minimum necessary levels. For example, in Madagascar the letters of credit were reduced by more than 50% in 1983, and documentary collections completely disappeared. Since 1987 with the improvement of the economic situation, the country has been able to go back on the market. But countries in this situation must also rely on other techniques to maintain their imports: cash collateral and countertrade or barter.

(b) The Institutional Factor.

The institutional factor played a key role in the availability of trade finance for Sub-Saharan African countries. Even within Sub-Saharan Africa the problem of short-term trade financing is different depending on the particular situation of each country:

> If a country is a member of the "Zone Franc", the situation remains manageable. Since the country has access to any foreign currency through the CFA Franc, the availability of trade financing depends only on the cash flow of the domestic bank offering the credit. In addition, in most countries of the "Zone Franc", the main banks dealing with trade finance are subsidiaries of large multinational French

banks. Hence, they still receive some lines from their headquarters to improve their liquidity. Therefore they still provide, albeit less than in the past, some short term financing to importers. In this zone, short-term trade lines were cut only in countries where the banking system went almost bankrupt.

For countries outside the "Zone Franc" it is more difficult to get access to trade financing. As in the case of "Zone Franc" countries, they still rely on credit lines granted by multinational banks to their subsidiaries in the countries. In case of real problems, the only recourse that remains involves more exotic techniques such as barter or countertrade which are often much more expensive.

The situation described above is still valid for most of Sub- Saharan African countries but, as in most of these countries, their financial situation is worsening, and some multinational banks are beginning to close their subsidiaries. This has been true for U.S or British banks which were less involved in Africa, but it is becoming true also for French Banks trying to withdraw from some small countries. If this situation continues to spread over Sub-Saharan African countries, short term financing to these countries could, indeed, be very difficult to obtain and the flow of imports could become even smaller then it is now.

(c) The Cost and Maturity Factor.

Besides the decreasing volume of classical short term trade financing, Sub-Saharan African countries also suffered a dramatic increase in the cost of trade lines associated with L/C. Depending on their funding on the Euro-market, trade lines are charged on the basis of a spread over LIBOR rate in a similar manner to traditional medium term Euro-credit. However, margins charged by banks on trade lines can vary in a very large range between countries, or for the same country. Generally, the spreads charged by banks have varied between 1/2 and 9% (on a yearly basis). Our discussion with involved parties has revealed that some of the main determinants the cost of trade lines are:

- The present financial and economic situation

- The relations with official international community (adjustment program or not)

- The prospects for the economic situation of the country in the next two years.

- The track record of past relations with bankers (moratorium, rescheduling of short term lines, among others)

- The size of the country and its political or strategic importance.

- The size of its industries and the importance of foreign trade.

These factors have been examined, among others, in the quantitative analysis that was performed for this study. Details of the study and results obtained are discussed later on in this paper.

To know the real price paid by LDCs remains difficult because there are often hidden charges imposed by banks to provide trade lines to a country. The present situation of some LDCs is typical. In one African country the cost of trade lines is officially LIBOR +3/8, and the maturity of trade lines have been stretched to as much as 18 months. Bankers did not want to extend trade lines at this price (i.e LIBOR +3/8) considering the growing risk of of further rescheduling of short term lines . In fact bankers agreed to extend new lines on the basis of LIBOR + 5%. However, the country did not want to pay more than the official price (LIBOR

+3/8), probably for political reasons, bankers increased the price via an alternative channel. An agreement was reached between bankers and exporters wherein banks would maintain trade lines at LIBOR +3/8 but would receive a commission from the exporters on the price of the goods exported. In reality, the banks are receiving the equivalent of LIBOR +5% from the country on the cost of its imported goods. This technique is widely used in the commercial and financial relations between OECD countries and LDCs. A country in Asia, for example, during the worst period of its financial crisis during the seventies, paid as much as LIBOR + 15% through this method of obtaining short term trade financing. This technique might partly explain why a recent World Bank study showed a higher average price paid by African countries on imports of selected goods from OECD countries than that paid by other LDCs.

The attitude of banks regarding the cost of trade lines also depends on the size of a country and on its potentialities. For a big country in a difficult financial situation they will cut few trade lines but charge a higher price, as was done in the case of Brazil. On the other hand, for small low-income countries such as those in Sub-Saharan Africa, they will cut most short term lines or even put a stop to their commercial relations.

Banks have a more pessimistic attitude toward trade lines since the inception of the debt crisis. They feel trapped in the rescheduling process and short term lines have been " de facto " transformed into long term lines. In addition, the terms of rescheduling are not significantly better than those for medium and long term debt. [The table in Annex 3 shows the cases where trade lines were specifically incorporated in commercial banks rescheduling agreements, and the terms on these rescheduled lines.] Nevertheless, it is clear that if these countries need new trade lines, they have to pay much higher margins. On the following table we present some of the spreads over LIBOR paid by some countries on short term trade lines by the end of 1989, on specific operations:

TABLE 3: Cost of Short Term Trade Financing.
Examples for Selected Countries

Country	Spread over LIBOR	Maturity
Brazil	3–4	Up to 1 yr.
Colombia	1 1/2	Up to 180 days
Cote d'Ivoire	3–4	Up to 180 days
Ecuador	1 1/2	Up to 180 days
Madagascar	2	Up to 180 days
Mexico	7/8	Up to 1 yr.
Mozambique	6	Up to 180 days
Venezuela	2	Up to 1 yr.

Source: Various Commercial Banks

(these figures are only example given by some important multinational banks on specific deals. They give us an idea of the average prices paid.

The evolution of trade lines in specific countries depends on the evolution of their financial situation. A good example can be given with what happened to Brazil after the authorities decided to declare a moratorium on commercial debt service at the end of 1986:

- Trade lines were cut by US$ 1.5 to 2 billion

- The spread on trade lines was increased from an average of 2-3% to an average of 3-6% over LIBOR.

- The maturities of all trade lines that were not subject to government restrictions were reduced from a maturity of 180/360 days to 30/60 days.

- Import financing was substantially reduced and most Brazilian importers had to operate on a cash basis during the period of the moratorium.

To face this situation, Brazil had to maintain a larger trade surplus, to deplete international reserves, and it probably suffered a negative impact on investment. A study by the World Bank shows that the cash flow impact for the country would have accumulated to US$ 3.5 billion over the year and the financial cost may have averaged US$ 500 million. It must be noted that, as soon as Brazil announced an interim financing agreement with commercial banks (end of 1987), short term lines were quickly restored.

Brazil could face this difficult situation because its financial system is almost as developed and efficient as in most industrialized countries. Thus, it was able to find ways to finance exports and exports, at least temporarily and at a higher cost. For most of Sub-Saharan African countries, most banks would have completely cut trade lines to the country, and they would have been unable to maintain current levels of foreign trade.

2. The Emergence of Other Techniques

53. As the global economic situation in Sub-Saharan Africa worsened during the last few years, commercial banks became more and more reluctant to provide traditional trade financing through letters of credit. Therefore, countries have relied more and more on other techniques such as prefinancing of exports, barter and countertrade, cash collateral. These techniques accounted for less than 5% of total trade financing during the 70's, they might now be averaging 20% of the trade financing. If there is no foreseeable improvement in the financial system in the next few years, this figure could increase even more.

The prefinancing of exports

When countries have no access to traditional trade lines as in the case of most IDA countries, pre-export financing is a way to keep trade going. In most cases, this technique is the last defense before recourse to very expansive techniques such as countertrade or barter. In general, pre-export financing lines are collateralized by commodity exports. For example, an exporter of cocoa in the LDC arranges for credit to finance his working capital requirements from a foreign financial institution by pledging a certain quantity of cocoa to the bank, or its assigned beneficiary (say, a cocoa importer in the OECD country), in the future at the time the crop is harvested. In some cases, the LDC exporter has also had to negotiate a preferential price at which the cocoa would be sold to the foreign bank or its assigned beneficiary at the future date. The cost of these lines have been relatively low until recently. The table below gives an idea of the spread charged on prefinancing of exports in several African countries by the end of 1989.

TABLE 4: Cost of Pre-Financing of Exports
Selected Countries

Country	Spread over LIBOR	Product Pledged
Cent. Afr. Rep.	2	Coffee
Cote d'Ivoire	0.4	Cocoa
Kenya	0.75	Coffee
Madagascar	1.25	Cotton
Zimbabwe	7/8	Coffee

Source: Various Commercial Banks

As Sub-Saharan African countries are mainly commodities producer, this technique has been of growing importance during the last few years. Lines provided by banks for pre-export financing were widely used for financing imports. Nevertheless, this technique is not the panacea. In prefinancing of export, trading companies are often part of the deals. Banks can provide the financing but the technical aspect of trading is done by trading companies. In these deals there are still several risks (quality of products, delivery, timing, etc.). These risks are generally taken on by banks. As the economic situation in a country worsens the above risks can increase, and banks will not want to provide this financing even with higher spreads and the country will have to rely on the most expansive techniques. Indeed, some IDA countries in Sub-Saharan Africa have reached this point.

Countertrade and Barter

Generally speaking, countries relying on these techniques are the poorer ones whose economic and financial situation is particularly bad, therefore, they have no choice. Often they are in a very weak position to negotiate and must accept very high spreads to get a deal. Countries working with these techniques are mostly African, but also include some Asian and Latin American nations. Information on this business is scarce, one reason being that profit can be very high and sometimes cover purposes other than pure traditional trade financing. An example of such an operation realized with an IDA only Sub-Saharan African country in 1987 shows some aspects of the problems raised by this type of financing.

This country which had no access to regular credit lines concluded an agreement with two commodity traders and an international bank for a countertrade operation. The operation relied on a coffee/oil deal. It can be described as follow:

- The International bank opened a US$ 50 million oil facility to be used by the country to purchase crude oil. This facility could be drawn against oil shipment. Each time an oil shipment was completed, oil documents were presented to the bank for payment.

- At the same time, the coffee board of the country entered into a coffee selling agreement with four established commodity brokers. Under the agreement, the coffee board of the country had to sell 50% of its coffee at auction in a normal way and 50% to the four brokers at a price calculated with a formula based on London and New York prices, adjusted for grade and other market factors.

- Net proceeds had to be paid into a coffee account with the international bank, and was available for a public bank of the country, to draw. In fact this money represented a guarantee on the oil facility granted to the country.

This mechanism is a typical countertrade operation in which the import facility (oil facility) is secured by proceeds from the export of commodities. Officially the fee charged by the bank seemed reasonable (Banker's acceptances rate + 1 3/8 %). The fact of the matter is rather different because the prices paid for oil and coffee differed from market prices. Under this agreement, the country accepted to pay for its oil imports at a rate 28.2% above the spot market price of oil and it received for its coffee a price of about 10% less than the market price. In this case this country ended paying a real fee amounting to about 25% of the facility conceded.

As can be seen in the above example, the cost of countertrade operations seems to be very high. From several interviews we had with bankers and traders involved in this business, we reach the conclusion that these prices are realistic. For most people involved in this business, fees of between 15 to 20% can be considered normal. This explains why some countries who relied on these techniques between 1983 and 1985 are now trying to finance their trade in a more orthodox way by improving their current economic situation and their relations with bankers.

The Technique of Cash Collateral.

Importing with cash collateral is a very simple technique. If an importer cannot obtain CILC from a bank he can send cash to a banker that authorizes the delivery of goods upon receipt of the money. In this case neither the banker nor the exporter have any risk. The banker realizes the settlement with the exporter and is responsible for the fund transfer and the bank draft. It must be noted that in this case, even with no risk, the bank takes a commission that has amounted in some operations with some Latin American countries, to between one and two percent of the value of the order.

The technique of export with cash collateral is still often employed for trading in a lot of countries. This technique was widely used in Latin American countries, as residents of these countries used their capital outside of the countries to maintain their level of imports. This has been the case for Argentina, and is still the case of Peru. In Africa this technique seems to be much less used, but a number of countries appear to have relied on it during critical periods.

3. ANALYSIS OF TRADE FINANCING TO LDCs

Having acquired "market" information on the techniques of commercial short-term trade lines to LDCs and understanding the possible complexity of the structure of each transaction, it is quite clear that any quantitative analysis of the determinants of short-term trade financing to LDCs will not be precise. However, this does not rule out the possibility of conducting a study in which one could get a general understanding of the factors that may be important in determining the quantity of short-term trade lines that commercial banks would make available to a country at any point in time. A more precise study would require a loan by loan analysis which is beyond the scope of this paper due to the confidential nature of most of the information on short-term trade lines from commercial banks and the limitations that exist with the few published sources of data on this subject. This also partly explains why very little work has been done on this subject in the past. It may also be useful to choose a few countries for which extensive time-series data on short term non-guaranteed trade credits is available and critically examine the behavior of short term lending by banks over time. This would enable us to track the dynamics of short term trade financing to LDCs. However, this is beyond the scope of this paper.

With this in mind, we embarked on a cross-section study of thirty-two countries, which consisted of the seventeen highly-indebted countries and fifteen low-income countries in Sub-Saharan Africa for which data was readily available as of December 1987. The countries were selected so as to provide a broad range of experiences within the wide spectrum of debt- distressed countries.

Methodology

The objective of the cross-sectional econometric analysis was to determine the factors that influence the amount of short-term trade lines that commercial banks would make available to less-developed countries at any point in time. In doing so it was our endeavor to find an answer to the question of whether a country's access to short-term trade lines is hampered in any way when it proceeds with a commercial debt-reduction operation. This was carried out by running alternative linear multivariate regressions with estimates of the amount of short-term trade lines to each country as the dependent variable.

The choice of factors to be examined (i.e. the independent variables) was decided on the basis of our "market" information on what commercial banks take into account when they extend short-term trade lines to a developing country. In this context several hypotheses were tested namely:

- How important are debt service ratios, such as the ratio of total debt service to exports of goods and services or the ratio of total debt outstanding and disbursed to Gross National Product (GNP), in determining a country's access to short-term trade lines from banks?

- Does the existence of a current Bank or Fund adjustment program matter? What about past adjustment experience?

- Some banks mentioned that they looked at the ratio of commercial bank debt to total debt outstanding and disbursed as a creditworthiness indicator in determining whether to extend short-term trade lines to a country or not. This hypothesis was tested.

- How important was the international reserves situation of a country in determining access to short-term trade lines. (cash collateral)?

- The "a priori" notion that the higher the trade deficit the more short-term trade lines a country would need and get was tested.

- Several aspects of commercial bank debt restructuring agreements were examined, e.g. Did the existence of a London Club agreement in any way influence a countries access to trade lines? The presence of such an agreement represents the existence of a previous long-term dialogue between the country and its commercial creditors. They may make it easier for them to get short-term trade lines. But, then again, if short-term trade lines have been converted/rolled over to medium and long-term loans in a recent restructuring agreement, this would not improve a country's access to short-term trade lines.

- If a country has officially declared a moratorium on its commercial bank debt service payments, e.g. Peru and Brazil, this would drastically reduce access to short-term trade lines. This hypothesis was also statistically tested.

- The influence of the secondary market prices of a country's sovereign commercial bank debt was also examined.

- Finally, a major component of any demand/supply function is the price. In this case the spreads over the London Inter-bank Offer Rate (LIBOR) which were charged on the short- term trade lines on a country were examined. Given the complexity of pricing of short-term trade lines and the unreliable data available at this point in time, the results obtained, especially for this variable, should be treated with caution. "A priori", one would think that as short-term trade lines become costlier the amount borrowed by countries would decline. However, several observations were brought to light during our interviews with involved parties in the market. It was suggested that the casual relationship between price and quantity of short-term trade lines may not only be one way. Once a certain quantity of short-term trade lines is requested by a country the bank may then determine what the cost of these lines would be. The risk premium on these trade lines may be charged as an up-front fee instead of a higher spread over LIBOR. In addition, if the transaction for which the short-term line of credit is required is very essential to the country's trade, it may have no choice but to pay the higher rate of interest to the bank providing the trade lines. This is particularly true for low-income countries in Sub-saharan Africa which are in arrears to commercial banks.

Alternative Estimates of Short Term Trade Financing

In view of the status of the published data on short-term trade finance to LDCs, which has been briefly described in Section 1 of this paper, none of the data sources provided a precise estimate of short-term trade finance from commercial banks to LDCs.

Therefore, we proceeded with our analysis with a "proxy" estimate of short-term trade finance. This measure was constructed to be an estimate of pure short-term trade lines from banks using DRS, World Bank data. Given the lack of any consistent and comparable series on the level of short term trade credits available to any country (especially those in Sub-Saharan Africa), any quantitative analysis on this subject would have to be done by using proxy estimates. The choice of an appropriate proxy will, of course, have biases associated with it. Therefore, any results that follow from the econometric analysis will depend on which proxy was selected to measure the flow of short-term trade lines to a country.

In our analysis, we begin with the premise that short-term trade lines are used to finance the non-capital goods component of a country's trade deficit. That is, the consumer goods and basic necessities that are imported from OECD countries are assumed to be financed by short-term trade lines. As the discussion in the previous sections on this paper revealed, it is not appropriate to look only at the value of imports of the LDC to get an idea of the level of short-term trade lines available to it at any point in time. The complex techniques of trade financing that are being currently used often effect the price and volume of exports of the LDC to an OECD country (countertrade, barter, and pre-financing of exports, among others). In this study, our objective was to identifying the primary determinants of short-term financing from banks to LDC The proxy estimate (henceforth STTLEST1) was computed by multiplying the trade deficit of a country in end-1987 (denominated in U.S. dollars) by the share of its non-capital goods imports the same year. In computing this estimate of short-term trade lines the following assumptions were made:

(i)   The entire trade deficit in that year would be financed by external borrowing.

(ii)   Capital goods imports are financed by medium and long-term borrowing while non-capital goods imports (mainly food, fuel and essential consumer goods) are financed by short-term trade lines from commercial banks.

Hence, it is implicitly being assumed that the component of the trade deficit that is due to non-capital goods imports is financed by short-term trade lines from commercial banks.

All information that was analyzed for the sample of thirty-two developing countries was a snapshot of the situation on December 31, 1987. For some countries, especially those in Sub-Saharan Africa, these are the latest available estimates.

Results of the Analysis

Given the quality of the data on short-term trade financing to LDCs and the need to use a proxy measure for the levels of such financing on a given year, any conclusions derived from the analysis should be treated with caution. The determinants of short-term trade financing from commercial banks were examined by running multivariate linear regressions for the estimates of the amount of short-term trade financing that were computed for the sample of thirty-two debt distressed countries. The cross-sectional analysis was carried out for data as of December 1987. The regression results are summarized in Table 5. These results should be interpreted more as statistical associations rather than a causal relationship between the left-hand-side variable and the right hand side variables. The current specification of the linear regression model is not enough to establish true independence of both sides of the equation. Therefore, the next step may be to define an alternative model with separate behavioral expressions for the supply and demand for short-term trade lines and estimate each equation simultaneously. Alternatively, some other proxy measure of the level of short term trade lines could be adopted. Nevertheless, we did get some interesting results using our proxy estimate (STTLEST1) which, to a large extent, supported the "market" information we had acquired.

The regression models run on Estimate I (STTLEST 1) of short-term trade lines clearly shows that the ratio of commercial bank debt to total debt outstanding and disbursed; the existence of a current Fund adjustment program; the magnitude of the trade deficit and international reserves situation of a country are significant determinants of the amount of short- term trade lines that will be available during a given year from commercial banks. Whether trade lines were included in past restructurings or not was also an important factor influencing a country's access to short-term trade lines. All these factors were statistically significant at the 5% level of significance. The current status of World Bank adjustment programs was statistically significant at 10% level of significance but not at the 5% level. However, the past track record of Bank adjustment (past five

TABLE 5: Determinants of Short-term Trade Lines from Commercial Banks Regression Results

Dependent Variable: STTLEST1				(Estimate I of Short-term Trade Lines)			
Variable				Coefficient Estimates			
Name CONSTANT	RCBTDOD	BADJCUR	FADJCUR	TRDEF	INTRES	TLINREST	MORAT87
MODEL IA 285.98 *	-2050.73 * *	239.38 *	-289.00 * *	0.63 * *	0.13 * *	522.88 * *	-323.11 *
(1.75)	(-2.65)	(1.75)	(-2.59)	(10.7)	(4.04)	(3.03)	(-2.05)
MODEL IB 427.16 *	-2262.67 * *	238.78 *	-290.60 * *	0.62 * *	0.14 * *	609.40 * *	-394.77 *
(1.97)	(-2.81)	(1.75)	(-2.60)	(10.42)	(4.13)	(3.15)	(-2.28)
MODEL IC 45.95	-2121.89 * *		-349.10 * *	0.64 * *	0.15 * *	638.97 * *	-363.37 * *
(0.25)	(-3.73)		(-3.14)	(12.56)	(5.18)	(4.21)	(-2.55)
MODEL ID 147.79	-3372.52 * *		-395.20 * *	0.66 * *	0.18 * *	901.55 * *	-463.65 * *
(0.64)	(-4.11)		(-3.49)	(12.43)	(5.73)	(4.72)	(-2.97)
MODEL IE 58.55	-3133.51 * *		-396.69 * *	0.66 * *	0.17 * *	784.67 * *	-357.20 * *
(0.24)	(-3.73)		(-3.30)	(11.7)	(5.32)	(4.37)	(-2.34)
MODEL IF 526.76 *	-1688.84 * *	260.40 *	-283.31 * *	0.58 * *	0.12 * *	493.79 * *	-329.02 *
(2.0)	(-2.70)	(1.95)	(-2.62)	(10.5)	(4.05)	(2.96)	(-1.96)

Computed by Author

** = Statistically significant at 5% level.

* = Statistically significant at 10% level.

Notes: Numbers in parentheses represents t-ratios.

Variable Name	SMP87	GEOG	SPREAD	BADJ5	CBREST2	CBDTRED3	R^2 (Adj.)
MODEL IA	2.49 (0.83)	-213.75 (1.25)					0.869
MODEL IB	3.32 (1.07)	-244.58 (-1.41)	-107.89 (-0.98)				0.869
MODEL IC				419.72 * (2.04)			0.880
MODEL ID	5.67 * (1.92)	-213.64 (1.49)	-130.47 (-1.29)	562.72 * * (2.63)			0.889
MODEL IE	3.97 (1.29)	-194.7 (-1.29)		558.14 * * (2.47)	-4.01 (-0.03)	-87.99 (-0.80)	0.877
MODEL IF		-226.2 (-1.33)	-94.48 (-0.88)		-54.7 (-0.41)	-92.20 (-0.86)	0.883

years) seemed to be more important in determining the amount of short-term trade lines that was available to a country.

As expected, the declaration of a moratorium or commercial bank debt service payments had a negative impact on the availability of short- term trade lines. In two regressions this factor was statistically significant at the 5% level but was significant in all four regressions at the 10% level of significance.

The ratio of commercial bank debt to total debt outstanding and disbursed indicates the degree of exposure of commercial banks in a country. Our results show that as this ratio rises, a country's access to short-term trade lines from commercial banks will be drastically reduced. This is represented by the large size of the coefficient estimates of the regressions and their negative sign. This result illustrates the "burden sharing" issue which banks brought to our notice, i.e., they would like to reduce their exposure in countries where the share of commercial bank debt to total debt was very large. They want official creditors to lend more to these countries instead.

The existence of a Bank adjustment program did have a positive impact on the availability of short-term trade lines for a country. The Bank's adjustment program, therefore, acts as a signalling mechanism to indicate the effort being taken by a country to implement economic reform in the pursuit of growth and development. When the Bank adjustment record of the past five years was incorporated in to the analysis, the positive effect on future access to short-term trade lines was much more significant. This would indicate the importance commercial banks place on Bank adjustment experience of a country over the medium-term Fund adjustment was a very important factor in determining short- term trade lines, but the impact was negative. It might very well be that the adoption of a Fund adjustment program indicates severe short-run balance of payments difficulties for the country. This would have a negative impact on the assessment by the banks of the repayment capability of the country during the short-run. Therefore, the quantity of short-term trade lines made available to a country under these circumstances would be less than would have been available to them when they were not perceived by the banks to have any short-run balance of payment difficulties, "ceteris paribus."

As expected, short-term trade lines were directly related to the trade deficit of a country. However, the coefficient estimates were not very large in magnitude. Similarly, the international reserves situation of a country was taken into account by banks in determining the amount of short-term trade lines to make available to it, "ceteris paribus," but the magnitude of the coefficient estimates were not very large.

The secondary market price of a country's sovereign debt was included in the regression because it was believed that they indicate the creditworthiness of a country and expectations about future repayment. This implies that the higher the secondary market price, the higher the probability of repayment (as perceived by the market) and more easy access to short-term trade lines from commercial banks. This conjecture was tested in our analysis. The sign of the coefficients was indeed positive but only in one of the regressions with this estimate of short-term trade lines (STTLEST1) did this factor turn out to be statistically significant at the 10% level.

The spreads over LIBOR at which short-term trade lines were extended were, indeed, negatively related to the amount of short-term trade lines borrowed by a country. However, this factor was not statistically significant even at the 10% level. This observation could be explained by the fact that, in several instances, the relationship between the cost of trade financing and the amount made available by banks is not one sided. It may very well be that once the country requests a certain amount of short-term trade lines, the spread is then determined by the bank on a case-by-case basis. The risk premium on these trade lines may be charged as an up-front fee instead of a higher spread over LIBOR. On the other hand, if the transaction for which the short-term trade lines is required is very essential to the country, it may be coerced to pay a higher rate to the bank providing the trade line.

The coefficient of the dummy variable which was used to flag countries in Sub-Saharan Africa in each regression was negative but not statistically significant. This negative bias of commercial banks towards these countries may be due to the fact that most banks would like to pull out of LDC lending, in general, and from Sub-Saharan Africa, in particular. It should be underscored that this factor did not turn out to be significant in determining the amount of short-term trade lines that were made available to a country by commercial banks at any point in time.

The regression results for the dummy variable representing situations where short-term trade lines were specifically entered into commercial bank rescheduling agreements was very interesting. Coefficient estimates of all the regressions were positive and the factor was significant at 5% level of significance. Our discussions with bankers have revealed that the inclusion of trade lines in reschedulings is not appreciated by banks, since they would be treated similar to medium- and long-term loans and may never be repaid but rolled over once again. This is especially true for small countries where new trade-lines could even be cut-off completely in the short-run when past trade-lines are included in rescheduling agreements. Available evidence shows that (except for Mozambique) short-term trade lines were rescheduled/refinanced for the highly-indebted countries which already had a very large amount of short- term trade lines outstanding from commercial banks. The positive coefficients of the dummy variable (TLINREST) could then be interpreted to show that trade lines would only be included in bank restructuring agreements if the amount of short-term trade lines being extended to a country by commercial banks is large in absolute terms. For countries in Sub-Saharan Africa, the inclusion of trade lines in rescheduling agreements could very well lead to a drastic reduction in access to new trade lines. In the very short-run they may even be cut off.

In addition, the positive sign may represent the positive impact of consolidating all commercial bank debt and charging uniform terms or reconciled numbers. The rescheduling may, therefore be looked upon as a positive step by the country to reconcile it figures with its commercial bank creditors and in this way improve future debt management.

To get a more reliable result regarding this factor it may be meaningful to evaluate the effect of each component of a bank rescheduling agreement on the future access to short-term trade lines. This can only be done on a case-by-case analysis of countries over time. However, the cross-sectional "snapshot" data as of a certain date does conclusively prove that the inclusion of trade lines in bank rescheduling agreements is a very important factor in determining future access to short-term trade lines from commercial banks.

4. CONCLUSIONS AND RECOMMENDATIONS

The objective of this study on short-term trade lines from commercial banks to developing countries was threefold:

- To improve our understanding of the mechanics of short-term financing.

- To get a sense of the impact of the debt crisis and deteriorating economic conditions on the access to short-term financing for the countries in Sub-Saharan Africa.

- To identify some of the key elements that were common across countries in determining the amount of short-term trade financing that is available to a country at any point in time.

The Reality of Trade Financing in Sub-Saharan Africa

The economic crisis of Sub-Saharan Africa and subsequent debt crisis had very unfavorable consequences on its relations with commercial banks. Most of the medium and long-term credit from commercial banks to the continent has been cut. However, its consequences for the countries has been somewhat curtailed by the fact that the private medium and long term financing has been substituted by public funds, from both bilateral and multilateral sources. The picture is rather different for short term trade financing for which few public substitutes were found. Therefore, these countries suffered a dramatic decline in their access to short term trade financing, and a marked shift from some techniques (the less expensive and complicated) to others which much more expensive and complex.

- Letters of credit almost disappeared from most of these countries.

- Most financing came from prefinancing of exports.

- In the less developed countries, they had to rely on exotic techniques such as barter or countertrade.

Some countries suffered less than others because they were members of the Franc Zone, and were not as exchange constrained as others. Countries needing hard currencies had much more problems financing their trade. The consequence of this situation was a dramatic increase in the cost of financing, a limitation of access to financing with probable implications on trade figures. From a long term development point of view, it is essential that these countries improve their access to trade financing (both in terms of amounts and cost) to be able to acquire necessary imports and develop its exports.

The results of our quantitative analysis clearly indicate that a moratorium on debt service payments has a significant negative effect on the amount of short trade lines a country would have access to at any point in time. In addition, the secondary market price for a country's medium and long-term commercial bank debt not very important in determining the cost and availability of short term trade lines from banks. The other conclusions of our econometric analysis support our initial findings on the basis of our survey of the limited literature on this subject and our numerous interviews with those involved with trade financing to LDCs in their day-to-day activities. It should be noted, however, that due to the lack of reliable accurate data in published sources, these empirical results were derived on the basis of "proxy" estimates of the amount of short term trade lines that were available to a country at a point in time. Results should, therefore, be treated with caution.

Recommendations for Improving Access to Short Term Financing

Our examination of the role and cost of trade financing in LDCs in general, countries of Sub-Saharan Africa, in particular, has shown that, the adjustment process is a prerequisite for any improvement. In economic stagnation or worsening of the economic situation, in some African country multinational banks have followed a policy of closing of subsidiaries in some African countries. This policy could accelerate the negative consequences on the availability and cost of trade lines from banks. The existence of an effective banking system can provide the technical skill necessary to any trade financing. Multilateral organizations can provide such assistance to these countries by providing some assistance to improve the technical capacity of the banking system (public or private).

The question remains as to whether it would be appropriate to design new financial products targeted to attract trade financing. In addition, should some third-party guarantee/enhancement scheme be formulated with the help of donors and multilateral institutions to bring the fees down? Further work has to be done in this context.

ANNEX I

List of Variables Used in the Econometric
Analysis of Trade Financing

Variable Name	Description	Source
STTLEST1	Short-term trade line estimate 1.	CFS Estimate using World Debt Tables, World Bank Country Briefs & The World Development Report, 1989.
RCBTDOD	Ratio of commercial bank debt to total debt outstanding and disbursed.	BIS Statistics of External Indebtedness (semi-annual), Jan. 89.
RDODXGS	Ratio of total debt outstanding and disbursed over exports of goods and services.	World Debt Tables, 1989.
BADJCUR	Current adjustment program with the Bank (1987).	CTRMI, World Bank FDB database,1989.
BADJ5	Adjustment program with the Bank over the last 5 years (1982-87)	CTRMI, World Bank FDB database, 1989.
FADJCUR	Current adjustment program with the Fund (1987).	IMF, Treasurer's Department, 1989.
RTDSXGS	Ratio of total debt service to exports of goods and services.	World Debt Tables, 1989.
RDODGNP	Ratio of total debt outstanding and disbursed to GNP.	World Debt Tables, 1989.
TRDEF	Trade deficit	Computed from the World Debt Tables, 1989 as difference of exports and imports.
INTRES	International Reserves	World Debt Tables 1989.

SPREAD	Spread over LIBOR charged by commercial bank first to that country.	CFS, World Bank.
SMP87	Secondary market price of sovereign bank debt in Dec. 1987.	Salomon Brothers
MORAT87	Declaration of moratorium on debt service payments to commercial banks between 1985 and 1987.	"Commercial Banks' Restructuring and New Money Facilities Agreements", CFS. World Bank, July 6, 1989.

ANNEX II Table 1: Trade Finance Data Used For Econometric Analysis

(as of December 1987)

Country	% Non K Goods * T Deficit	ST Bank Claims (OECD)	Comm. Bank Debt/Tot. Debt (%)	Bank Adj. Prog Current	Fund Adj. Prog Current	5 yr. Bank Adj. History	Comm. Bank Restruc. Past 2 Yrs	DS Ratio TDS/XGS	DOD/GNP
CNTRY	STTLEST1	STTLEST2	RCBTDOD	BADJCUR	FADJCUR	BADJ5	CBREST2	RTDSXGS	RDODGNP
Argentina	3,549.9	840	0.58	1	0	1	1	45.3	61.7
Benin	218.4	76	0.19	1	1	0	0	15.9	56.5
Bolivia	369.6	377	0.10	1	1	1	1	22.1	110.8
Brazil	1,003.8	9,251	0.56	1	1	1	1	26.7	29.1
Cent.Afr. Rep.	120.9	5	0.03	1	1	1	0	12.0	49.2
Chile	695.3	2,910	0.60	1	1	1	1	21.1	90.8
Colombia	83.2	316	0.37	0	0	1	1	30.7	40.8
Costa Rica	309.8	413	0.29	0	1	1	1	12.1	88.8
Cote d'Ivoire	200.5	1,304	0.03	1	1	1	1	19.6	89.5
Ecuador	731.6	537	0.51	0	0	1	1	20.7	92.9
Guinea-Bissau	46.1	2	0.05	1	1	1	0	37.1	321.3
Honduras	263.2	223	0.20	0	0	1	1	23.0	70.6
Jamaica	161.3	158	0.11	0	1	1	1	25.8	138.9
Kenya	455.0	512	0.21	1	1	1	0	28.8	57.9
Madagascar	247.5	126	0.06	1	1	1	1	35.5	168.4
Malawi	65.0	26	0.06	1	1	1	1	23.3	92.7
Mali	184.8	35	0.02	1	1	1	0	9.9	95.7
Mauritania	113.9	58	0.05	1	1	1	0	18.2	215.1
Mexico	0.0	14,861	0.65	1	0	1	1	30.1	59.9
Morocco	313.6	2,042	0.25	1	1	1	1	23.4	118.1
Mozambique	433.0	118	0.07	1	1	1	1	227.7	270
Niger	109.0	49	0.15	1	1	1	1	33.5	60.4
Nigeria	65.3	5,771	0.38	1	1	1	1	10.0	109.8
Peru	752.1	4,153	0.23	0	0	0	1	12.5	28
Philippines	732.2	2,504	0.44	1	1	1	1	22.7	64.5
Poland	0.0	5,140	0.28	0	0	0	1	14.3	55.7
Tanzania	442.6	194	0.08	1	1	1	0	18.5	143.7
Togo	102.8	116	0.09	1	1	1	1	13.9	90.7
Uruguay	113.5	571	0.55	1	0	1	1	24.4	42.2
Venezuela	186.7	5,216	0.69	0	1	1	1	22.4	65.3
Yugoslavia	530.3	1,822	0.42	0	1	1	1	13.3	23.9
Zaire	497.7	387	0.12	1	0	1	1	12.8	139.5

Notes: 1. For countries where the spread over LIBOR charged by banks on short-term trade lines is not available a spread of one percent is assumed.

2. For countries that had a trade surplus in end-1987 (Mexico and Poland) STTLEST1 was assumed to be zero.

ANNEX II

Country	Trade Deficit	Internat. Reserves	Imports	Comm.Debt Reduction 1985-87	Trade Lines incl. in Resched.	Spread over LIBOR	Sec. Mkt. Price (Dec.87)	Moratorium on Comm. DS (85-87)	Location
CNTRY	TRDEF	INTRES	IMP	CBDTRED3	TLINREST	SPREAD	SMP87	MORAT87	GEOG
Argentina	4,277	3,734	5.82	0	1	0.81	33.5	0	0
Benin	260	9	0.63	0	0	1.00		0	1
Bolivia	616	530	0.78	1	0	1.00	11.0	0	0
Brazil	1,375	7,477	16.58	0	1	0.88	46.0	1	0
Cent.Afr. Rep.	195	102	0.10	0	0	3.20	60.0	0	1
Chile	927	3,244	3.79	0	1	1.38	61.0	0	0
Colombia	130	3,416	4.32	0	0	1.00	65.0	0	0
Costa Rica	413	519	1.38	1	1	1.00	15.0	1	0
Cote d'Ivoire	257	30	4.61	0	0	0.40	40.0	1	1
Ecuador	1,092	692	1.99	0	1	1.63	36.5	0	0
Guinea-Bissau	64	0	0.09	0	0	1.00		0	1
Honduras	329	114	0.90	0	0	1.00	22.0	0	0
Jamaica	224	174	1.21	1	0	1.00	33.0	0	0
Kenya	711	294	1.76	0	0	0.75	96.0	0	1
Madagascar	330	185	0.33	1	0	1.00	50.0	0	1
Malawi	89	58	0.30	0	0	1.00	45.0	0	1
Mali	330	25	0.45	0	0	1.00	13.5	0	1
Mauritania	146	77	0.24	0	0	1.00		0	1
Mexico	(3,217)	13,692	12.73	1	1	1.88	50.0	0	0
Morocco	397	752	3.85	0	1	1.19	52.0	0	1
Mozambique	528	148	0.74	1	1	1.13	8.0	1	1
Niger	158	254	0.35	0	0	1.00	57.5	0	1
Nigeria	102	1,489	7.82	0	1	1.25	29.0	0	1
Peru	1,419	1,319	2.91	1	1	1.00	7.0	1	0
Philippines	882	2,312	7.14	0	1	1.75	50.0	0	0
Poland	(800)	1,723	11.24	0	1	1.81	42.8	0	0
Tanzania	835	32	0.92	0	0	1.00	16.0	0	1
Togo	137	361	0.30	0	0	1.00	39.0	0	1
Uruguay	132	1,793	1.14	1	1	1.88	59.0	0	0
Venezuela	263	11,511	9.54	1	0	1.00	57.0	0	0
Yugoslavia	707	1,602	11.34	0	1	1.88	49.0	0	0
Zaire	790	417	0.76	1	0	1.00	19.0	0	1

ANNEX III - Finance Conditions for Trade Credit Negotiated in Past Rescheduling Agreements.

COUNTRY	1983	1984	1985	1986	1987	1988
Argentina			L + 1 3/8		L + 13/16	
					CD + 13/16	
Brazil	L + 1 3/8	L + 1		L + 1 1/8		L + 5/8
Chile	L + 1 1/2		L + 1 3/8		L + 1 3/8	
	P + 1 3/8		P + 1 1/8		P + 1 1/8	
Costa Rica			L + 1 3/4			
			P + 1 5/8			
Cuba	L + 1 1/4	L + 1 1/4	L + 1 1/8			
Ecuador	L + 1 5/8			L + 1 3/8	L + 1 5/8	
	P + 1 1/2				P + 1 1/4	
Mexico				L + 13/16	L + 7/8	
Morocco			L + 1 3/4		L + 1 3/16	
Mozambique					L + 1 1/8	
Nigeria	L + 1 1/2	L + 1			L + 1 1/4	L + 1 1/4
	P + 1 3/8					
Panama			L + 1			
Peru	L + 1 1/2					
	P + 1 1/4					
Philippines			L + 1 1/4		L + 3/4	
Poland		L + 1 7/8			L + 13/16	
Uruguay	L + 2 1/4			L + 1 3/8	L + 7/8	
	P + 2 1/8					
Yugoslavia	L + 1 3/8					
	P + 1 1/4					

Source: World Bank

NOTE: L = LIBOR

P = PRIME

CD = Certificate of Deposit

BIBLIOGRAPHY

"Attractions of financing trade paper" INTERNATIONAL FINANCIAL LAW REVIEW (U.K.) 5, pg.8-13, July 1986.

Bowen, David, "Trade Finance in Britain -- The Consumer's View", EUROMONEY TRADE FINANCE REPORT (U.K.) No. 26 pg: 33-28, June 1985.

Chase Trade Information Corp., "International Trade Financing: conventional and nonconventional practices", 2nd. ed. New York, 1981.

Eisemann, Frederic, Bontoux, Charles, and Rowe, Michael(eds.), "Le credit documentaire dans le commerce exterieur : commentaire reglementaiton uniforme internationale et formules normalisees", Paris: Jupiter 1985.

Giscard d'Estaing, Francois."Financement et garanties du commerce international", Paris: Presses universitaires de France, 1977.

Gmur, Charles J.(ed.), "Trade financing", 2nd. ed. London: Euromoney Publications, 1986.

Gmur, Charles J. and Budd, Nicholas (ed.), "Case histories in trade financing", London: Euromoney Publications, 1984.

Gmur, Charles J. "Un credit management efficace en tenant compte du forfaitage, du leasing et du factoring", Zurich: Finance SA, 1983.

Guild, Ian. and Harris, Rhodri, "Forfaiting: an alternative approach to export trade finance", Cambridge : Woodhead-Faulkner ; 1985.

Hall, Michael. "Export Finance", BRITISH BUSINESS (U.K.) 21:26-27, April 4, 1986.

Hammond, Grant Tedrick, "Countertrade, Offsets and Barter in International Political Economy", London: Pinter Publishers Ltd.. 1990.

International Chamber of Commerce, "Uniform customs and practice for documentary credits", 1983, rev. ed. New York, N.Y.: International Chamber of Commerce.

Jones, Stephen F. and Jagoe, Ashley, "Third World Countertrade", U.K.: Produce Studies Ltd., 1988.

Kingman-Brundage, Jane. and Schulz, Susan A.,"The fundamentals of trade finance: the ins and outs of import-export financing", New York: Wiley, 1986.

Knight, Martin. and Ball, James. and Ingliks-Taylor, Andrew(eds.), "Export finance", 1988. London: Euromoney Publications. 1988.

"Le rachat de creances", MONITEUR DU COMMERCE INTERNATIONAL (FRANCE) No. 718:15-30, June 30, 1986.

Louberge, Henri and Maurer, Pierre (eds.), "Financement et assurance des credits a l'exportation : aspects theoriques et pratiques en vigueur dans les pays europeens", Geneve : Librairie Droz, 1985.

Lowenfeld, Andreas F. "International private trade", 2nd. ed. New York: M. Bender, 1981.

Mills, Dominic, "USA: Trade finance means taking the country risk", Euromoney Trade Finance Report, UK: No. 42, pg. 25-45. October 1986.

Rowe, Michael, "Countertrade", U.K.: Euromoney Publications PLC, 1989.

Rowe, Michael. "Using letters of credit in trade", INTERNATIONAL FINANCIAL LAW REVIEW (U.K.) 5:29-31, March 1986.

Schneider, Gerhard W. "Export-Import Financing: A Practical Guide", New York: Wiley, 1974.

Euromoney, "Trade financing: the official agencies; how the consensus survived", EUROMONEY (U.K.), January 1984.

Usunier, Jean-Claude. "Environment international et gestion de l'exportation", Paris : Presses Universitaires de France, 1985.

Promoting Limited Recourse Project Finance to Developing Countries

Nirmaljit Singh Paul

CONTENTS

PROMOTING LIMITED RECOURSE PROJECT FINANCE TO DEVELOPING COUNTRIES

INTRODUCTION

This report examines project finance[1] from commercial banks to developing countries, with a view to identifying possible areas of involvement by interested parties, including official parties, for promoting project finance flows to these countries. It discusses traditional project finance techniques and the attributes of viable project finance. It examines impediments to growth in project finance flows to developing countries and describes innovative financial and legal structuring and other techniques that could be used to facilitate these flows. While the paper addresses general difficulties encountered by developing countries in accessing project finance, it also discusses the special problems of highly indebted countries.

For highly indebted countries that appear to be recovering from the debt crisis, the paper examines possible project finance mechanisms for facilitating the eventual restoration of access to financial markets on a voluntary basis. The return to creditworthiness is likely to be long and arduous, and requires sustained economic and debt servicing performance by the debtor countries to re-establish creditor confidence. These countries could, nevertheless, benefit from the support of interested parties in reintroducing their "name" to the financial markets. The debtor countries are likely to gain access first to trade-related and other short term finance, and then to project finance--particularly on a limited or nonrecourse basis--before gaining access to general purpose term finance.

---

1   The paper focuses on limited recourse project finance from commercial bank sources alone. Project finance from other sources including export credit agencies, other official entities, bond market sources, equity and quasi-equity financing sources and risk capital sources is beyond the scope of this paper. In this paper, the term "project finance" refers to the financing of a particular capital project in which a lender looks initially to the earnings and cash flows of the project for repayment and servicing of a loan and to the assets of the project entity as collateral for the loan. The general credit of the project sponsors is not directly relevant because the financing is without recourse (or with limited recourse) to them.

1. COMMERCIAL BANK FINANCE TO DEVELOPING COUNTRIES

The last two decades have seen major institutional changes in the provision of development finance. From the oil shock in 1973 to the inception of the international debt crisis in 1982, the international market for bank loans gradually replaced the markets for international bonds and direct investment as the major source of development finance from private sources (see table 1 and charts 1 and 2).

The aftermath of the oil shock of 1973-74 and the ensuing international payments imbalances led to an unprecedented expansion of the credit markets. There was a considerable increase in the supply of financial resources in the oil-exporting countries, which was met by an increasing demand for financing in the non oil-producing developing countries, to meet inflated oil-import-related payments obligations. These payment imbalances led to two major institutional developments that heavily influenced the international bank market to assume the principal role of channelling oil surpluses to the developing countries. The second oil shock in 1979 and the resulting oil surpluses accelerated this trend.

The first development was a reduction in risks on bank deposits, as the official sector in the developed countries (deposit insurance agencies, central banks and other government agencies) gradually assumed a substantial portion of the default risk of the deposit liabilities of commercial banks. Second, several financial and legal innovations lowered the perceived overall risk of bank lending to sovereign borrowers, through sharing among lenders of the risk and responsibility in lending, and perceived increases in the cost of default to the borrower.

Sharing of risk and responsibility among the bank lenders came about through loan syndications, under which many individual lenders subscribed to portions of loans, while each was protected with regard to repayment through sharing, mandatory prepayment, pari passu and other clauses in loan syndication agreements. The introduction of cross-default clauses in loan agreements reduced the perceived differences in the credit risk of individual (usually public sector) borrowers within a country, as potentially delinquent borrowers were supported by other borrowers to prevent default (Cross-default clauses prevented individual borrowers within a country from defaulting without the entire country being declared in default.) Public guarantees of private sector debt also contributed to the homogenization of the risk in borrowers within a country.

The effect of these innovations was to raise the perceived cost of default for the borrower in terms of denial of future access to international banking markets, and disruption of relations not only with the international financial community as a whole but also with individual industrial countries. In a broad sense, the effect was to shift some of the risk in sovereign lending from bank lenders to national financial authorities in industrial countries and to the developing countries.

Such institutional developments, combined with significant increases in the supply of loanable resources and intense competition among banks, were key factors responsible for the unprecedented growth in the international bank market during the 1970s and early 1980s.

Growth in Project Finance

There was also growth in commercial bank lending for projects during this period. Banks shifted away from balance-of-payments loans and toward project finance-- where loan agreements provided that repayments would be tied to the cash flows generated by the project with limited or no recourse to other income or assets of the sponsor. Bankers realized that a project-oriented approach could significantly reduce the problems in balance-of-payments loans because: (1) Assessments of project risks would be simpler since lenders could focus their credit analysis on a self-contained business entity, (2) repayment uncertainties would be reduced, as the lenders would have a specific source, the project's earnings, to look to for repayments, and (3) through loan negotiation and participation in the structuring of the security package, lenders would be able to exercise some control over the planning and management of the project, reducing the likelihood of project failure and loan default.

There were several benefits, too, from the standpoint of the borrowers- sponsors of the projects. Project financing helped free up the sponsors' borrowing capacities. It also allowed them to engage in ventures requiring larger amounts of financing than they were otherwise capable of or willing to undertake. Through the limited recourse feature, they were able to transfer most of the project risk to lenders and third parties.

The inception of the international debt crisis in 1982 marked the beginning of a new phase in international bank lending in which sovereign lending from private sources to developing countries declined substantially. The decline in lending to highly indebted countries was even more dramatic. Medium- and long- term general purpose (balance of payments) finance from commercial banks to highly indebted countries on a voluntary basis ceased almost completely. Preserving the value of the existing claims on developing countries, and postponing the day of reckoning, became the principal objectives of banks as they scrambled to accumulate reserves to protect their balance sheets against potential losses. Thus bank lending became concerted and involuntary. Voluntary lending activity was restricted to trade-related and other short-term finance, which was also adversely affected--albeit much less seriously--as trade lines were cut, price spreads were inflated and secured financing as a share of total lending was increased.

Subsequently, under the Baker Plan, concerted lending from commercial banks and financial support from the official sector were provided to support economic adjustment and growth in the debtor countries. This was premised on the assumption that, given appropriate economic policies, financial support for implementing those policies, and adequate time for intensification of adjustment efforts, the debtor countries would grow out of their debt problems. This period saw several developments, primarily in response to the evolving needs and constraints of debtors and creditors as they continued to muddle through, while avoiding confrontation, and attempted to reach negotiated resolutions. These developments included the introduction of the multi-year restructuring agreements, lengthening of tenors and grace periods of restructured debt, and the evolution of the market-based menu approach.

The Brady Initiative, launched in the spring of 1989, recognized the need for debt and debt service reduction as an essential element in the menu of options under a debt restructuring package. During 1989-90, four countries--Mexico, Philippines, Costa Rica, and Venezuela--negotiated external debt restructuring packages with their commercial bank creditors under the Brady Plan; several more are now negotiating agreements. For some of these debtors, the worst payments difficulties seem to be over and, with continuing economic adjustment efforts, they appear to be on the path of economic growth, creditworthiness, and the restoration of normal access to voluntary finance.

Reasons to Support Project Finance

While prospects look promising, the return to creditworthiness in all likelihood will be long and arduous. Creditors will be more cautious in resuming lending to these countries, given their debt servicing track record. A sustained economic and debt servicing performance by the debtor country will be required to re-establish creditor confidence. Indeed, full restoration of access to voluntary finance from commercial banks may not be possible for a number of years for many countries. Even the general purpose finance in significant amounts may be unavailable.

The importance of private finance in development cannot be overstated. The resources of the official sector that can be devoted to development are simply too small. In the absence of general purpose finance, two main types of private finance available to the developing countries are short-term finance and project finance. The debtor countries are likely first to gain access to trade-related and other types of short-term finance. Beyond that, they are likely to gain access to project finance, particularly on a limited or non-recourse basis, before eventually gaining access to general purpose term finance.

2. PROJECT FINANCE

Essentially, there are two principal ways in which debt finance can be raised by a commercial entity: through a conventional borrowing under which the lenders have full recourse to the borrower for repayment of principal and interest; and through the receipt of the principal of a loan as the "price" for the use or sale of an asset, under which the lenders have no recourse (or limited recourse) to the sponsors-owners beyond the asset itself. The term "project finance" is not generally associated with the former technique, even though the borrowing may be made in the context of a project. It is the second method that characterizes project finance.

In essence, in project finance lenders look initially to the earnings and cash flows of the project for repayment and servicing of the loan and to the assets of the project entity as collateral for the loan. Lenders have no (or limited) recourse to the project sponsors for the repayment or servicing of their loans. Through security packages and risk distribution mechanisms, however, the recourse of lenders with regard to certain risks may subsequently be shifted to guarantors, sponsors and other parties.

Sources of Project Finance

Maturities and sources of finance are generally matched to the specific requirements of a project. Long-term requirements are financed by long-term sources, and medium- and short-term requirements by the medium- and short- term sources of finance available to the project entity.

The principal medium- and long-term sources of finance are private investors (ordinary and preferred shareholders), commercial banks, investment banks, bond markets, risk capital sources, export credit agencies, multilateral and bilateral agencies, lessors, and suppliers and buyers. Short-term finance includes trade credits, suppliers and buyers credits, working capital loans, and commercial paper.[2]

Attributes of Viable Project Finance

To qualify for private finance, a project must be commercially viable. This means that the project must be technically and financially viable and supported by strong credit. Project financing must also take into account political, economic, and social factors, and the design of security packages must provide sufficient protection against the possible adverse effects of these factors on project operation and earnings.

Risks in Project Finance

The risks in a project can be classified by their nature as well as their timing in the project cycle. The former can be further broadly classified as general commercial risks, political or country risks, sovereign risks, and risks related to foreign investment in developing countries.

(1)   Commercial. General commercial risks include the risk of cost overruns caused by increasing input costs, rising financing costs and general inflationary increases; of delays in construction; of

---

2   This list is by no means exhaustive. Financing for projects can also be obtained from other sources through a variety of techniques.

declining demand for outputs in the absence of long-term purchase contracts; and force majeure risks.

(2)   Political. These include risks of expropriation, of increased government interference through increased regulation, higher taxes, and restrictions on the export of the project output and the import of project input. Political instability in developing countries can increase the risk of civil unrest, terrorism or war. Furthermore, there may be currency convertibility (transfer risks) and other foreign exchange risks. The political system weaknesses and adverse socio-economic conditions generally endemic to developing countries lead to significant political risk.

(3)   Sovereign. This is different from political or country risk in that it refers to the risk inherent in loans to a sovereign nation by foreign lenders. It is related to the borrowing country's ability and willingness to fulfill its foreign currency payment obligations.

(4)   Specific Risks in Highly Indebted Countries. The indebtedness problem in highly indebted countries poses additional risks. Since foreign exchange resources are scarce, the most significant risk is currency convertibility. Moreover, many highly indebted countries suffering from deep structural economic distortions have political and socio-economic problems intertwined with the indebtedness problem. These can affect, directly or indirectly, many of the project's operating parameters, and pose significant risks. Finally, specific regulatory, accounting, and tax factors governing commercial bank lending to highly indebted countries present additional costs and burdens for the banks.

The risks in project finance can also be classified by the different phases of the project cycle: that is, by the construction or pre- commissioning phase, the startup or commissioning phase, and the post-commissioning or operational phase. Some risks are specific to one or two phases, while others are present in all phases. Clearly, in each phase both commercial and political risks are present.

In the construction phase, the principal risks are delays in commencing construction; cost overruns and delays arising from force majeure of contractors or suppliers, damage in transit or on site, or bankruptcy of shareholders or suppliers; failure to complete required infrastructure arrangements on schedule for any reasons, including force majeure; and government intervention leading to escalation of construction costs and delays in commissioning. Start-up risks are mainly technical difficulties in commissioning, due, inter alia, to failure of plant and equipment to perform to specification; labor unrest; and commissioning delays with associated cost increases and revenue losses. During the operational phase there are risks of shortfall in input supplies, shortfall in the level of sales, low output prices, and higher-than-expected inflation levels. Finally, the following risks are present in all phases of the project cycle: foreign exchange risk, risk of cost escalation due to increases in interest rates, currency convertibility risk, failure by shareholders to honor cost overrun sharing commitments, and the risk of nationalization, expropriation and other forms of government intervention.

Guarantees to Distribute Risk

The challenge of structuring viable project finance is to devise a financing and security package which is in line with the sponsors' principal objectives and gives lenders an acceptable degree of risk. Risk spreading mechanisms allow the risks to be distributed among sponsors, lenders, governments and interested third parties so that an acceptable allocation of risk results.

A traditional instrument is a guarantee of the indebtedness of the project company. Guarantees permit off-balance sheet financing by sponsors who may be constrained from borrowing more; and they enable promoters to shift the risk among interested parties who may otherwise be unprepared to finance the project directly.

Guarantors

Typically, parties extending guarantees in project finance are either owners-sponsors or interested third parties.

Owners-Sponsors. Governments, parent companies of controlled subsidiaries, foreign and domestic investors in joint ventures, and other owners-sponsors of projects may provide guarantees for the indebtedness of the project company. These guarantees are generally required by lenders when the project company has inadequate capital or operating track record to support indebtedness on the basis of its own financial standing.

Interested Third Parties. This important and varied group includes:

(1) Sellers of equipment and supplies. Parties interested in selling equipment or supplies, or leasing a plant or equipment to a project, are generally willing to extend guarantees. For example, a company eager to dispose off excess equipment may guarantee a project which would need such equipment.

(2) Suppliers of raw material and intermediate goods. Suppliers may be motivated to extend guarantees by the prospect of an ensured market for their product once the project facility is operating. Suppliers might also benefit from the use of the new processing facilities created under a project which may boost the sales of their product.

(3) Users of project output. Demanders of the final output of the project may extend guarantees or direct financing to help assure the needed supply. For example, these might include users of primary commodities interested in an ensured supply of raw materials.

(4) Construction Firms. Contractors engaged in a project are generally in the construction business and may be willing to provide guarantees and other forms of support, to promote their business interest.

(5) Host country governments and international agencies. These entities are motivated by economic, political, and social needs of the host country. Government guarantees may be necessary to cover project risks which are simply not covered by other participants and hence may be critical to the success of the financing.

(6) Other Parties. Often there are other parties that benefit from the construction of a project and may be therefore willing to extend guarantees. For example, a company with existing operations near the project site may benefit from the infrastructure developed for the project as well as from local economic expansion the project may create.

Types of Guarantees

Guarantees may be broadly classified as direct or indirect guarantees. These may include the following.[3]

Direct Guarantees. Guarantees are usually direct and unconditional undertakings which, in the case of default, transfer the responsibility for all payment obligations due to the lender from the guaranteed party to the guarantor. In project finance, however, lenders themselves are willing to bear certain types and degree of risk, and hence a partial, rather than a complete, guarantee is often sufficient. Partial guarantees may be extended by sponsors or third parties to cover certain risks (for example, political risk and force majeure risk), while lenders bear other risks (such as commercial risk).

(1) Cost overrun guarantee. In general, lenders are willing to finance a project if the costs are predictable. For this reason, they insist on cost overrun guarantees by the sponsors or interested third parties-- to the extent, of course, that this risk is not covered by a completion guarantee. Cost overrun guarantees are limited with respect to the amount of the liability.

(2) Completion guarantee. This is the most basic guarantee limited with respect to time. Since the period of greatest risk is the construction and commissioning phases of a project, sponsors provide completion guarantees to protect the lenders. Guarantors undertake to complete the project within a certain period of time and to extend financial resources to cover all cost overruns, irrespective of cause. In this sense, completion guarantees provide "full recourse" for the lenders during the construction and startup phases of a project.

(3) Contingent guarantee. Lenders often require that others cover risks that, although remote, would be very costly. Such guarantees generally cover events beyond the control of the parties participating in the financing, such as an unanticipated change in price, government action, civil unrest, or war.

Indirect Guarantees. Lenders typically bear the commercial risks during the operating phase of the project. However, they may demand protection against factors which are beyond the control of the project participants and which could affect the project's ability to generate earnings to service its debt. Often an indirect guarantee is used to assure a minimum stream of project revenues. The most common guarantees of this type are take-or-pay contracts, through-put contracts, and hell-or-high-water agreements.

---

[3] This is not an exhaustive list.

(1) Take-or-pay contracts. Under a take-or-pay contract, users of project output, sponsors, or third parties agree to make periodic payments in return for a given portion of the project's output. The obligation to make payments is unconditional, regardless of whether the product or service is actually delivered.

(2) Through-put agreements. Similar to take or-pay contracts, these agreements are usually found in pipeline projects. They stipulate that the pipeline users put a minimum amount of product through the pipeline at periodic intervals and pay for the use of the pipeline, irrespective of whether the stipulated amount of the product is actually put through or not.

(3) Hell-or-high-water agreements. These are essentially the same as take-or-pay contracts. They are generally appended to leases under which customers guarantee to use the facilities owned by a project company for which they will pay, come "hell-or-high-water."

Other Techniques to Distribute Risk

Although the guarantee is the predominant method of spreading risk, it is not the only one. Other means frequently used are forward purchase agreements and production payments.

Forward purchase agreements. In a typical case of forward purchase (sometimes called "advance payment") financing, the lender makes a loan to purchase minerals or other resources which have not yet been delivered or produced. When the project begins operating and the minerals are produced, the lenders have the right to take quantities equivalent to the scheduled debt service on the loans.

Production Payments. This method involves the purchase by the lenders for a principal sum, a portion of the future production of a project. It differs from forward purchase agreements (FPAs) in that the stream of future payments depends on actual production rather than a fixed schedule of payments under FPAs. Used typically in mineral mining projects, the production payment is usually secured by an interest in the natural resource in place. When production eventually begins, the purchaser-lender receives its share of income based on a predetermined portion of the output each period.

Hedging, insurance, and swaps. These techniques and mechanisms are employed by the participants in a project finance to further adjust the risk that has been allocated to them, with a view to finding a more appropriate match with their preferred risk-reward profile. Each such technique has a cost associated with it, which must be factored into the risk-reward tradeoff.

3. IMPEDIMENTS TO PROJECT FINANCE

As discussed above, project finance generally involves a wide variety of risks; it involves additional risks when the borrower is a developing country. Political risk is considerable, and even more so for a highly indebted country. The success of project finance depends on matching these risks to the risk-reward profiles of all the participants. This matching is typically done by tailoring the financial and legal structure of the financing to the specific risk characteristics of the project. If risks cannot be allocated appropriately, the financing is not feasible.

Over the past few months, Bank staff surveyed selected commercial banks on their attitude toward project finance to developing countries. For developing countries in general, the principal findings are as follows:

- Commercial banks appear interested in limited and non-recourse project finance in developing countries including, to an extent, highly indebted countries.

- In general, banks are likely to participate in projects oriented towards exports. Of particular interest are export-oriented projects with gross revenue pledges (export proceeds are received in an offshore escrow account, from which operating expenses and selected capital expenses are deducted first, and then debt service payments are made, before the residual is paid to project sponsors). Domestic projects generating revenues in local currency involve risks related to the availability of foreign exchange for servicing the debt (i.e., transfer risks). Banks are generally reluctant to bear these risks, particularly in highly indebted countries, irrespective of the project's commercial viability.

- Banks also want comprehensive political risk coverage with few exclusions. Banks generally feel that limited guarantees of political risk are inadequate in assembling financial packages on a commercial basis, particularly for highly indebted countries. Furthermore, political risk must be clearly defined. They are likely to be relatively comfortable if political risk cover includes at least the following: expropriation, war, labor unrest, and violation of foreign exchange contracts (currency convertibility, product exportability and so on).

- Regulatory factors and potential changes in the law of debtor countries are of considerable concern. For example, in Canada the Superintendent of Financial Institutions (SOFI) has set a mandatory minimum requirement of 45% reserves provision for loans to any of 42 highly indebted countries it has identified. Even in the case of financings involving no new money, such as debt equity conversions, some provisioning is required. Exceptions are made if the project has 100% guarantee against political risks by the Canadian Export Development Corporation or a 100% corporate guarantee against political risks by foreign sponsors or contractors involved in the project. At the same time, commercial risk must be covered by export revenues or third parties. The carrying costs of the required reserves, as well as tax obligations (although such reserves are tax deductible), raise the overall cost of financing projects, and thus impose a major constraint for banks.

- Commercial banks see the issue of government counter guarantees as potentially troublesome in formulating and assembling financial packages on a commercial basis. The reason is that banks traditionally view project finance as a private undertaking, and government counter-guarantees introduce a sovereign element to the package. Moreover, banks may be reluctant to participate in a project financing on a build-operate-transfer or build-operate-own basis, because of the usually extensive involvement of government in these projects, either directly through off-take contracts, or indirectly through the provision of services, pricing regulations, issuance of consents, and so on. In their view, the line between commercial and political risks in this context is difficult to discern and therefore would require unconditional guarantees in order to attract commercial bank financing; and

- Finally, banks also related difficulties with: (1) insufficient equity investment by sponsors-investors; (2) insufficient general sponsor commitment (for example, in the form of deficiency guarantees); and (3) obtaining appropriate off-take contracts.

For highly indebted countries specifically, we found that:

- Banks were fairly uniform in their view of participation in project finance. The banks distinguish between those highly indebted countries with improved prospects for resolution of the debt problem (such as Mexico, Chile, and to an extent, Venezuela), and those which still appear to have a long way to go (such as Argentina and Peru). For the former category, most banks felt that participation in project finance would be possible, if political risk[4] is adequately covered through official or other enhancements (such as sponsor guarantees). For the second group, however, they felt that voluntary new money finance, even on a limited recourse basis, is unlikely to be forthcoming in the foreseeable feature. Still, participation by banks as well as investors through debt-equity and debt-debt conversions is possible. Banks are eager to improve the quality of their assets by converting loan claims on the central bank, for example, to equity in a healthy public or private enterprise. The attraction for investors is the high return on investment due to the secondary market discount on debt.

- Regarding transfer risk, these banks prefer export-oriented projects with escrow arrangements but would be willing to participate in other projects as well, if the security package contains suitable protection against transfer risk.

- Most banks appear willing to assume commercial risk, but not political and transfer risk, for the less seriously indebted highly indebted countries. However, some banks pointed out that commercial risk cannot be completely delineated from political risk, particularly in highly indebted countries, where socio-economic and political factors can influence a project's commercial and operating parameters--such as availability and cost

---

4 For example, the Bank is constrained from providing credit enhancement support to the highly indebted countries. Under extant policy guidelines governing the Bank's ECO program, the Bank is restricted to providing ECO support only for countries that have not restructured their external debt during the last five-year period.

of labor, raw material, infrastructure services and other inputs, during both construction and operating phases of the project. This latter group of banks appeared less inclined to participate in financings in even less risky highly indebted countries.

- Banks generally would prefer debt-equity, debt-debt, or quasi-equity financing and are the least likely to provide new money.

4. TECHNIQUES FOR PROMOTING PROJECT FINANCE

For parties interested in promoting private sector project finance to developing countries there are two possible paths: one facilitating overall economic structural and institutional reforms in the developing countries, to create an environment conducive to greater project finance flows; the other is facilitating individual financing operations through direct involvement, cofinancing, credit enhancement support and other means. Briefly stated, the first includes, inter alia, macroeconomic reforms to ensure monetary, fiscal and external sector stability and balance, and sector reforms to develop infrastructure and reduce investment costs. It also involves rationalizing the financial system to remove distortions as well as to meet the needs of the private sector. This paper focuses on the second.

Many interested parties, particularly official ones, are constrained from providing credit enhancement or direct financing support to the highly indebted countries.[5] Thus, certain techniques specially applicable to developing countries may not be feasible for highly indebted countries. To analyze possible techniques for facilitating project finance, therefore, a distinction should be made between developing countries without serious debt problems and those with them, the highly indebted countries. In this section, we deal with each group in turn.

Support for Developing Countries Without Significant Indebtedness Problems

Both direct and indirect support to project finance operations could be provided by interested (and qualified) parties through: (1) arranging and packaging project finance, (2) providing "seed" finance, and (3) providing credit enhancement support for reducing risk.

Arranging and Packaging Project Finance: Structuring an appropriate security package is of the utmost importance in designing a viable project finance package. Interested creditworthy parties could have a role in arranging and packaging the financing from various sources, and allocating risk in ways that meet the needs of the financiers, sponsors and project beneficiaries. This would facilitate the assembling of the lowest cost, minimum risk financing packages. Clear demarcation of responsibilities for risk would remove uncertainties that often inhibit project finance.

When needed, foreign ownership and participation can be arranged through joint ventures with local enterprises, or through provision of technical and management services by foreign firms that may be interested in gaining experience in working in the recipient country before investing financial resources. The involvement of foreign entities would help the transfer of technology and management skills.

Providing "Seed" Finance. Projects often involve significant expenditures during the preappraisal and appraisal phases (and sometimes also during the construction phase), which are essential for the project to proceed but are not easily financed. These may include expenses for carrying out financial and technical feasibility studies, payment of interest during construction (unless this is capitalized), and initial working capital. Sometimes the security package of an otherwise viable project finance may require an initial

---

5   For example, the Bank Group can provide direct debt and equity financing (IBRD and IFC), as well as guarantees (IBRD, IFC, MIGA) to cover different types of risks. It can therefore have a lead role in arranging and packaging project financings to LDCs.

contribution from the host government who may be cash-constrained. In other cases, financiers may be unwilling to fund infrastructure components required by the project's remote location. Interested parties could provide seed finance through traditional forms of lending, parallel financing, or cofinancing. Finance could also be provided for buying insurance for the risks allocated to the host government, which the government may decide to hedge against and for which private insurance is normally available.

Providing Support for Risk Reduction. While commercial financiers are generally willing to accept commercial risk in a developing country project (with the possible exception of completion risks), provided the security provisions are adequate, they are typically unwilling to assume political risk (including the currency convertibility risk). But, lender and investor criteria for the acceptability of risk vary with the country and the project. In some cases, lenders-investors may be unwilling to accept certain commercial risks (such as product price and offtake risks). Or they may not be fully comfortable with the host government assuming these and other risks and may need to be reassured about the government's risk-bearing ability. Credit enhancement support for these risks--through guarantees, direct funding of contingency facilities, or other mechanisms--may be critical for the success of these financings. Even if it is limited, support from creditworthy parties can be significant in assuaging lender concerns. Possible types of support are as follows:

- Support of completion guarantees. Host government and other sponsors are typically required to bear the completion risks through completion guarantees which include cost overrun payment and other obligations. Interested parties can assuage lender concerns as to the government's ability and willingness to meet its obligations by guaranteeing the contingent commitments. Or they could provide a contingency facility to be drawn down in the event of a default by the government to honor its commitment under completion guarantee. Yet another type of support could be a guarantee of a contingency facility funded by the commercial lenders.

- Product price support. Project financing agreements typically involve formulas that reflect the price of the project output, including so-called price "floors." Lenders, however, often are concerned that purchasers of the output will not honor their commitments, particularly if the actual price falls below the floor value. When the purchaser is the host government, third parties could consider providing guarantees or other forms of support to cover the government's commitment under the project agreement.

- Support of output volume or off-take contracts. Where the host government is the purchaser of project output and lender are uncertain of its ability to meet its obligations, guarantees or other forms of credit support could be provided to cover the government's commitments under offtake contracts, or production payment agreements.

- Currency convertibility guarantees: Import substitution projects, which do not generate hard currency revenues, inherently carry the currency convertibility risk. The risk is lower in countries in good credit standing and without significant indebtedness. It is also mitigated, to an extent, if the government expressly assigns priority in its use of scarce external resources to the foreign exchange requirements of the project. Nevertheless, lenders' confidence, and hence the prospects of the project's success, could be improved by formal credit enhancement of this risk by interested parties.

- <u>Political risks</u>. Interested parties could provide coverage of specific political risks which are either uninsurable or cannot be accepted by third parties, but nonetheless must be covered as a condition for lender-investor participation. Interested parties could also provide a revolving guarantee covering periodic payments, up to a pre-determined ceiling, which could be affected by the overall creditworthiness of the government.

<u>Subordination of Other Debt</u>. The risk of a given category of debt can also be reduced by making this debt senior over other debt. For example, private lenders typically look for greater legal comfort and risk reduction than other lenders, sponsors, investors, and other interested parties. The latter group (parties other than private lenders) has other interests and stakes in the project and is therefore willing to accept subordinate status for their claims. Private source financing could therefore be imparted seniority over other pieces of the project finance to arrive at a workable security package.

Support for the Highly Indebted Countries

Some of the techniques for mobilizing project finance flows can clearly be applied in countries without significant indebtedness, but not all project finance techniques are possible for the highly indebted countries. While these techniques may facilitate coverage of some elements of political and other risks, they would not provide complete and satisfactory coverage--from the lender's perspective--of the special risks of project finance in the highly indebted countries. Hence, guarantees of residual risks may still be required. These guarantees could be extended by the official sector or other creditworthy parties. The more seriously indebted the country, the greater the need for such guarantees.

<u>Debt Conversions</u>. While commercial banks are likely to be disinclined to provide new money debt financing to highly indebted countries, they may be less averse to converting their existing debt exposure to project finance. Debt conversions could be used for providing equity, quasi-equity, senior debt, or other forms of financing for the project company.

<u>Debt Conversions with New Money Lending</u>. One drawback of simple debt conversion is that the resulting financing would essentially be in local currency. For projects with high import content and significant external financing component, this technique may be inappropriate. However, this problem could be partly addressed by requiring that debt conversions be accompanied by new money lending in some pre-determined proportion. The entire package may be sweetened by additional incentives and "kickers" such as preferential exchange rates for the conversions, preferential rights over domestic currency project revenues, preferential treatment for remittances of dividends and repatriation of capital, and onlending/relending rights.

<u>Debt for Developments Swaps</u>. Under the host country's debt conversion program, infrastructure and other development projects could be partially financed through conversions of existing commercial bank debt into local currency. Many official organizations and aid agencies are likely to support this type of project finance within the context of their development aid programs. Also, many private sector companies in the industrial countries may be interested in participating in such financings with a view to introducing their technology and capital goods in the host countries.

<u>Debt Repayments into Local Currency Project financing Pool</u>. Under this mechanism, debt service payments on existing commercial bank debt would be made in local currency into a fund to be used for financing investment projects in a highly indebted country. Banks interested in financing individual projects would use their portion of fund

resources to do so. Again, a certain level of external financing could be ensured by requiring new money lending in some pre-determined proportion.

Enclave Financing with Offshore Escrow Accounts. In foreign exchange generating projects, offshore trust accounts can be created. Foreign exchange earnings of the project would be deposited into these accounts, and debt service payments to the lenders would be made from the proceeds. Alternatively, the escrow proceeds could be used to set up a sinking fund for defeasance of the commercial bank debt. This mechanism would thus ensure that certain foreign exchange payment obligations of the project company would be met from resources outside its control, thereby minimizing the currency convertibility and transfer risk. Clearly, however, this mechanism would not provide protection against other political risks such as the imposition of new government controls on the export of the project output.

Build-Operate-Transfer (or Own). Under these methods the private sector is involved in the construction and operation of a project for a sufficiently long period to present a commercially attractive rate of return on investment. These methods also allow transfer of technology and managerial expertise. Since these project project finance techniques attract experienced and reputable contractors-operators, certain risks-- particularly commercial ones--are mitigated. Political risks still remain. Clearly, however, for this technique to be successfully employed, such issues as government counter- guaranties in the case of World Bank participation must be resolved.

Underwriting Note Issuance Facilities During the Operation Phase. This technique could be used to restrict the commercial bank exposure during the construction phase of the project. Under the mechanism, banks would provide loans during construction. These would be "taken out" at the end of the construction period through the proceeds of bond issues backed by export revenues held in offshore escrow accounts. Issuance of bonds would be facilitated by guarantees or backup underwriting facilities, to be provided by creditworthy third parties.

Financing Infrastructure Projects Near Project Site. Ultimately, the success of some major capital projects depends on development of infrastructure (road/rail links, communications, etc.) near the project site. Development institutions and other parties could facilitate by financing portions of the required infrastructure.

Parallel Financing and Complementary Financing. While some interested parties may be constrained from providing more formal types of credit enhancement for highly indebted countries, they may be less constrained by other mechanisms where, for instance, the legal link to cofinanciers is weaker. The comfort afforded to the lenders under these mechanisms might in some cases be adequate to produce a viable security package.

Sharing Payments under Enclave Financing. This technique could be used as a vehicle of support by creditworthy participants who provide direct financing to the project. Under enclave financing escrow account arrangements, interested parties could participate in a project through direct lending along with commercial banks. The escrow proceeds would be used to service third party and commercial bank loans pro rata.

The Reemergence of Developing Countries in the International Bond Markets

A Cofinancing Financial Advisory Services Study

Marcus J. J. Fedder
Mohua Mukherjee

CONTENTS

INTRODUCTION

The international capital markets never completely closed their doors to developing country borrowers. Even during the debt crisis in the 1980s amid difficult negotiations, restructurings and payment moratoriums, several developing countries were successful in their attempts to tap the international bond markets. Most countries remained excluded, however, and the majority of developing country borrowers who need external financing will not have access to these markets in the foreseeable future. Yet for some, the international bond markets have recently reopened. It is on these countries that our analysis will mainly focus. The study examines what influences the ability of different developing countries to tap the international bond markets. It concludes with a set of lessons and a suggested strategy for countries that have not obtained access to this market.

A part of the surplus savings from industrialized nations, as well as flight capital seeking high returns, has always flowed to developing countries, through direct foreign investment or through loans and bonds. Investors in developing country enterprises have usually sought to profit from the high returns earned in protected developing country markets, returns that often result from subsidized input prices, barriers to entry and other anticompetitive policy distortions, as well as a scarcity premium on foreign exchange. But, such investments have been limited in many countries by restrictions on direct foreign ownership. High-interest-bearing financial investments in developing countries have also proved generally profitable in the past, until the debt crisis of the early 1980s, when the excesses of general-purpose developing country loan syndications proved unmanageable for many sovereign borrowers.[1] Some developing countries that very recently experienced debt servicing difficulties are once again turning to the international capital markets, this time increasingly for bond financing.

The onset of the debt crisis was the first time in the past two decades that a clear distinction between the performance of loans and the performance of bonds became evident to borrowers and indebted countries alike. With few exceptions, even the most heavily indebted countries made it a point to continue servicing their outstanding sovereign bond obligations throughout the debt crisis.[2] Mexico, for example, repaid bondholders in full—exercising put options before maturity for at least two large public enterprise borrowers—and its recent bond servicing record has continued to be impeccable. Bonds constituted a small part (on average 5-8%) of the outstanding obligations of most developing countries. They were held by two groups: retail investors and institutions, which were for the most part located in the United States, Europe, and Japan. Servicing bond debt did not pose a large burden on the borrowers' foreign exchange reserves, and developing country policymakers consciously excluded bond debt from moratoria and reschedulings.

In addition to distinctions between the value of loans and the value of bonds as financial assets, sharp divergences in the inherent creditworthiness of different developing countries became apparent in the early 1980s. Despite faithful bond debt repayments, several (mainly Latin American) borrowers, whose access had seemed almost unlimited before 1982, were shut out from obtaining any voluntary financing. Other developing country borrowers (mainly Asian) never lost access and, in fact, sharply increased their bond market activities during the 1980s. A third group of developing country borrowers, the East European countries, maintained good debt servicing records and accumulated considerable external obligations.[3] Subsequent political changes, accompanied by the transition to market-based economies, have highlighted

---

1 See section 3 for a discussion of widespread developing country defaults in the 1930s, and differences in the profitability of dollar and sterling denominated issues.

2 Costa Rica, Panama and Yugoslavia are the exceptions.

3 Poland is an exception.

weaknesses and created serious doubts about this region's debt servicing capacity. But, with one exception, all bonds continue to be serviced punctually.[4] Czechoslovakia, which did not enter the Eurobond markets under its previous regime, is successfully tapping the Eurobond market already, only months after the installation of an elected government.[5] Hungary was the region's most active bond market borrower throughout the 1980s and continues as such, having recently pledged not to undergo any Brady-type restructurings despite financial difficulties.

What influences the presence of developing country borrowers in the international bond markets? Does bond financing represent a small but permanent window for additional funding to developing countries? Or is it for some countries a short-term, unstable opportunity to attract the savings of risk-prone investors who seek quick capital gains? We conclude that the markets are indeed ready to hold substantial amounts of paper of selected developing country borrowers. We also conclude that the Eurobond, Yankee, and Samurai markets together present a large, stable pool of funding and are potential sources of new money for those developing country borrowers that can gain access to these investors.[6] In a nutshell, a solid record of servicing previous bond issues, sound macroeconomic management, high yields (often double digit coupons), and securitized structures or government guarantees for introductory issues appear to be prerequisites for a developing country to have a successful market presence.

The analysis here focuses mainly on the issues that would affect strategies followed by those borrowers staging a reentry to the international bond market, after having lost access during the debt crisis in the 1980s. We present two middle-income country case studies—Mexico and Turkey. Mexico is a highly indebted borrower that lost access to all voluntary lending for most of the 1980s, negotiated significant Brady-type debt reduction on its outstanding obligations to commercial banks, and is already staging a comeback in the bond markets, though the voluntary commercial loan market remains closed. Mexico is remarkable since it has raised more than US$1 billion in various bond markets and probably even more in the short-term certificate of deposit (CD) market, all since June 1989. Turkey is a rescheduling country that underwent major debt servicing difficulties in 1978-81 but maintained uninterrupted (though rescheduled) debt service payments throughout the 1980s. Turkey became active in the syndicated loan market once more in 1984, when confidence was restored in the government's ability to adjust its economy and maintain payments. By 1987 this borrowing strategy had shifted to include Eurobond financing.

The study also covers several Asian developing countries that never experienced debt servicing difficulties and consequently never lost access to voluntary lending.[7]

This study deals with different groups of borrowers in three markets: the US domestic market, the Eurobond market (which has various currencies) and the Japanese Samurai and private placement markets. First, we will present a historical overview focusing on the developments of the 1980s, which is necessary to provide an understanding of current developments. For this purpose the borrowings of Asia, Europe, and Latin America, are briefly

---

4   Bulgaria, which stopped servicing yen private placements.

5   Czechoslovakia successfully completed two yen private placements in 1986.

6   Including yen private placement.

7   The information in this section has been researched and compiled from a number of sources, including 1986, 1988 and 1990 issues of International Capital Markets--Developments and Prospects, International Monetary Fund; selected editions of Global International Financing Review, and Dealing with the Debt Crisis, World Bank 1989.
    Discrepancies regarding the size of a particular bond issue or annual borrowing total were noted on several occasions in the different publications. It is assumed that these are due to exchange rate differences when borrowings in several currencies are aggregated in US dollar equivalents. Wherever possible, the most recently published information has been used. However, 1981 and 1982 data are taken from the 1986 issue of International Capital Markets published by the IMF since that was the only source available for these figures.

analyzed. We next raise the question of recent reschedulings and defaults and, for comparative purposes, give a brief history of defaults, concentrating on the interesting case of Brazil, which shows many parallels to today's situation. Then we briefly outline some macroeconomic considerations in reestablishing access to capital markets—a topic discussed in light of the respective experiences—and present certain debt related ratios for purposes of comparison. Last, we discuss the recent conversion bonds of the Mexican and Venezuelan Brady-type restructuring and their implications for the bond markets.

1. HISTORICAL OVERVIEW

Over the last two decades, there have been major institutional changes in the channeling of development finance. International payments imbalances following the oil shock in 1973 led to an unprecedented expansion of the credit markets. The increased supply of private funds from oil-exporting countries was used to meet an increased demand for financing by developing countries, resulting in part from their inflated oil-related costs. The international market for bank loans gradually replaced the markets for international bonds and direct investment as the major private source of development funds, until the onset of the debt crisis in 1982. All sovereign lending from nonofficial sector sources declined substantially, and medium- and long-term balance-of-payments finance from commercial banks to highly indebted countries on a voluntary basis ceased almost completely.[8] Voluntary lending activity was restricted to trade-related and other short-term, secured finance, so that total bond-issuing activities remained in the range of US$1 billion - 2 billion a year for most of the 1970s, peaking briefly in 1978 at US$3 billion - 4 billion. The second oil shock in 1979 and the resulting oil surpluses added further impetus to the intense competition among banks.

Developments in the 1980s

Up to the first half of 1986, there was a rapid increase in total net lending worldwide, accompanied by a continuing shift towards reliance on bond markets to finance these flows. Bond markets accounted for about 43% of net bond and bank lending during this period, compared with 13% in 1980-81.

Figure 1

Access to International Bond Markets by Category of Borrower

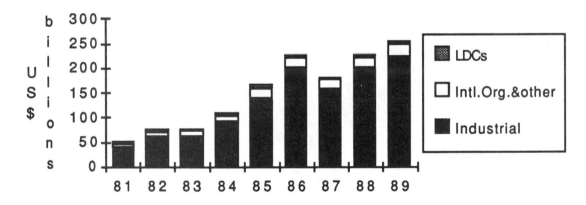

---

[8] N. Paul, " Possible Techniques for Promoting Limited Recourse Project Finance to Developing Countries World Bank." CFSFA, September,1990

Reasons for Increased Popularity of Bonds

Investors in industrial countries began to favor tradable assets heavily in the mid-1980s, and channeled funds through securities markets in far greater volume than through banks. A substantial decline in long-term interest rates, resulting in capital gains for bondholders, and the higher returns that could be achieved from bonds in comparison to those from time deposits or savings accounts also help to explain the increasing importance of the bond markets. A key factor in the expansion also came from the development and increased use of medium-term currency and interest rate swaps. The volume of interest rate swaps rose from only $20 billion in 1985 to more than $50 billion in 1986 and has since become a $1 trillion business. These instruments have enabled borrowers to tap markets with the greatest investor demand and yet to obtain funding in desired currencies. In addition, investor demand for fixed-rate bonds could be satisfied even when the borrower needed floating rate funds: interest rate swaps would simply convert a fixed-rate liability into a floating-rate obligation for the borrower.

This growth in securities transactions has however, been restricted primarily to an expansion of lending within the industrial country group. In contrast, the reduced external financing of capital importing developing countries has been largely met through sources other than international capital markets. In 1985, for example, borrowers from industrial countries accounted for 82% of the international bond market, followed by international organizations with 11% and developing countries with 6%; by 1989 the share of developing countries stood at only 2% of all international bond issues.

There was a sharp contraction in activity in the global international bond markets in 1987, followed by an expansion of 25% in 1988 to regain the peak level of 1986. The recovery continued in 1989, but was concentrated in equity warrant issues by Japanese borrowers, while other market segments were generally depressed.

Gross international bond issues registered a sharp increase in 1985 and continued to rise in 1986. At the same time, however, the number of developing countries tapping the bond markets fell from 22 to 18. Developing country bond issuers were highly concentrated during 1985-86, with eight developing countries from Asia and Europe accounting for 80% of the total value of such issues. Most developing country bonds are straight public issues, with 5-7 year maturities. Over 60% of the bonds issued by developing countries are floating-rate notes; these bonds may have been purchased largely by banks. Developing country bonds frequently have government guarantees, and they are issued in the names of public enterprises or government-owned banks. [9]

---

9 Korean bond issuers are always corporate entities, by contrast. Korean borrowers are also able to obtain the longest maturities and have frequently used equity warrant structures (thus reducing the coupon and the IRR of the bonds). Malaysian and Thai bonds up to 1989 have always been sovereign.

Figure 2

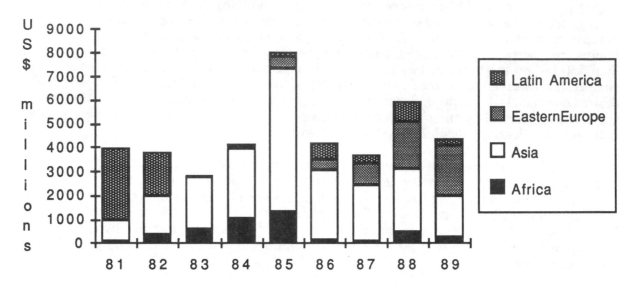

Geographical Distribution of LDC Bond Issues in the 1980s

Breakdown of Developing Country Issues in the 1980s

      Asia. Bond issues by developing countries in Asia totalled almost US$3 billion in 1984, US$6 billion in 1985 and almost US$3 billion in 1986. In 1985, Malaysia borrowed US$2 billion (of which 65% were in floating-rate notes), Korea US$1.7 billion, and China and Thailand almost US$1 billion each. India was the other significant borrower, with an issue of over US$400 million. Although reliance on the bond markets was reduced in 1986, it still remained about 50% above the average of 1982-84. China, Korea, India, and Indonesia were the principal borrowers in 1986. Thailand and Malaysia, both large issuers in 1985, together borrowed less than US$100 million in 1986. Bond issues continued to slow in this part of the world in 1987 to US$2.4 billion, compared with US$3 billion the previous year. Except Malaysia, which issued almost US$200 million more in 1987 than in 1986, borrowers reduced their bond issues relative to the previous year. China remained the largest borrower among all developing countries accounting for about one-fourth of all issues during 1986-87 and for almost half of the amounts placed by developing countries from Asia. Gross issues by Asian borrowers totalled US$2.6 billion in 1988, the bulk of which was accounted for by China, India, and Malaysia. The US$715 million of bonds issued by India in 1988 was its highest of the decade, and reflected a sharp increase over previous annual totals. In 1989, Asian borrowing declined by almost US$1 billion to US$1.7 billion, due largely to reduced borrowing by China (down to US$150 million from a 1988 total of over US$900 million). India and Malaysia were most active in 1989, with bond issues of close to US$593 and US$428 million respectively. China has been absent from the international bond markets in 1990/91. Korean corporations were the most frequent Asian borrowers in the capital markets throughout 1990, and in the first half of 1991 with issues of fixed rate US dollar and DM convertible bonds (of 10-15 years'maturity on average, in sizes of US$30-70 million).

Figure 3

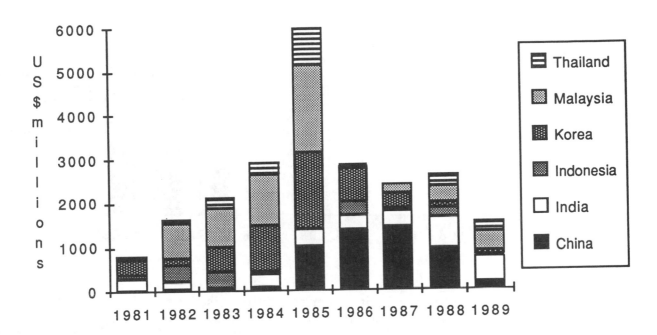

Breakdown of Principal Asian Bond Issuers in the 1980s

Europe. The principal developing country bond issuer between 1984 and 1987 in Europe was Hungary.[10] In 1988 it was overtaken by Turkey, which issued US$1.2 billion of a regional annual total of US$2 billion, with Hungary accounting for the rest. The two countries together borrowed slightly over US$2 billion in 1989. Turkey entered the international bond markets for the first time in 1985 with an initial volume of US$62.5 million. Both Hungary and Turkey have maintained a continuous presence in the international bond markets in 1990 and 1991. Details are provided in Annex Table 1.

---

10 Greece, Cyprus and Portugal were included under European developing country bond issuers from 1981-1983 in the IFR and OECD statistics. They have been deliberately omitted here because (a) they are no longer developing countries and (b) to focus attention on Turkey and Hungary.

Figure 4

Breakdown of Developing Country Bond Issuers in Europe in the 1980s

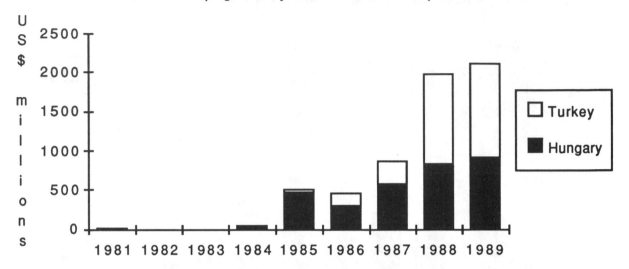

Latin America. Latin American borrowers were well represented in the international bond markets in 1981 and 1982, with Mexican issues accounting for almost US$4 billion of a combined Latin American total of US$4.7 billion for 1981-82. Brazil, Colombia, Mexico and Venezuela successfully tapped the markets in both 1981 and 1982; Argentina, Chile, and Peru issued their last bonds for the decade in 1981. The US$49 million equivalent bond issue by Mexico in 1985 was a foreign yen placement, the first of its kind since the debt crisis of 1982. Of the close to US$650 million in bond issues in 1986 for Colombia, Brazil, and Mexico combined, there were a number of note issuance facilities arranged for Mexico and Brazil to transform interbank lines into marketable securities. (This restructuring of interbank lines should not be confused with the later Brady bonds. Although no new money was added, as with normal Eurobonds or private placements, the investor base could thus be enlarged.) Argentina and Venezuelan bond issues from 1986-1988 are mainly new money bonds and transformations of existing obligations to commercial bank sources, whereas Mexican bonds in 1988 and 1989 represent securitized and other direct new issue deals (see Section 4). Among Caribbean borrowers, Barbados, Bermuda, Trinidad, and Tobago all tapped the international bond markets in the 1980s for relatively small amounts.

In 1990-91, Mexico, Venezuela, Chile and in token amounts even Argentina and Brazil have all staged a comeback to the bond markets. A private corporate Argentine borrower placed an unsecured five year, US$26 million fixed rate bond with an 11% coupon in December 1990. Chile issued a five year floating rate bond in March 1991 as part of a refinancing package for commercial debt. The state-owned Brazilian refinery PETROBRAS issued a two year unsecured US$250 million fixed rate bond in August 1991 with an effective yield of 13.5%. The bond is Brazil's first issue since the early 1980s, and contains a call option after one year. Venezuelan steel and petroleum companies have tapped the markets in 1990. Mexico is by far the largest Latin American issuer in the Eurobond markets, with a total of 19 new issues in 1990-91, totalling US$1.992 billion. PEMEX and government agencies account for about 40% of the borrowing, and the remainder is corporate. The spreads over US Treasuries have been narrowing in secondary market trading.

Figure 5

Breakdown of Principal Latin American Bond Issuers in the 1980s

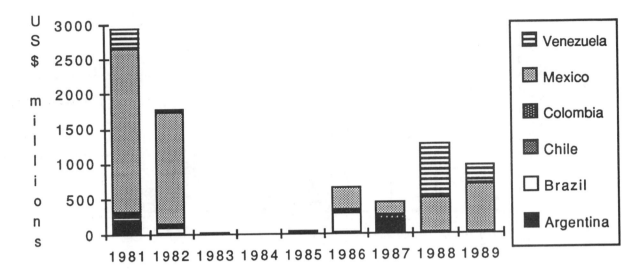

Africa. African borrowings are mainly limited to Algeria and South Africa. Algeria entered the market with a US$500 million issue in 1985 and tapped the DM market with three issues, totalling DM500 million, in 1986 and 1988; South Africa has been present throughout the decade and an issuer almost every year. South Africa's annual borrowing volume jumped from about US$100 million in 1981 to close to US$1 billion in 1984 and 1985 and then fell below US$40 million in 1988. Egypt issued about US$160 million in international bonds in 1982, 1983, and 1985. Among borrowers in sub-Saharan Africa, only Gabon appears to have tapped the market successfully in the 1980s, with a small Euro issue US$33 million in 1983.[11]

---

11 Not included in the graph.

Figure 6

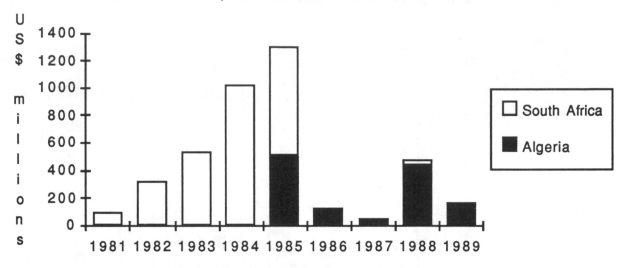

Breakdown of Principal Bond Issuers in Africa in the 1980s

Recent Reschedulings/Defaults in the International Bond Markets

Developing country bonds have traditionally been exempted from commercial debt rescheduling exercises. The few sovereign issues with debt servicing interruptions in the 1980s include Costa Rica, Panama, Yugoslavia and, most recently, Bulgaria in 1990. For Costa Rica, bonds were omitted from the 1982-83 rescheduling exercises but were part of the 1985 agreements, largely on the basis of burden-sharing arguments put forth by commercial banks faced with delayed payment of their claims. The bonds in question were three floating-rate notes with a total face value of $90 million. All were to mature in 1985 and were instead amalgamated into one new issue by means of global notes. The global notes were then exchangeable for so-called New Notes with semi-annual interest payments after April 15, 1986. The government contacted the holders of its bearer bonds (through advertisements in London newspapers) and offered two options: either participate in the 1985 commercial bank refinancing agreement, or accept the new conditions offered, which consisted of an average 5 1/2 year extension in maturity from the original bullet maturity in October 1985 and an increase in the spread over Libor from 7/8% to 1.25%. The obligor for the previous notes had been the Republic of Costa Rica. The Central Bank was to be the issuer and obligor for the New Notes, which did not carry an explicit guarantee by the Republic. The notes have since been serviced on schedule.

Of other bond issues subject to payments problems, Panama suspended payment on a $20 million FRN issued in 1985. Bulgaria issued one Eurobond in June 1989, a seven-year DM200 million straight public issue with a coupon of 8.5%, held mainly by German retail investors. This issue continues to be serviced despite a moratorium on all of Bulgaria's other external obligations since March 1990. In addition, there are four yen private placements, amounting to Y31 billion, which are held by Japanese banks and institutional investors, one of which was issued early in 1989, just before the DM Eurobond. It appears that these yen private placements are no longer being serviced. If this is so, then the most likely explanation is that the Bulgarian authorities responsible for the debt believed the effect of suspending service on bonds held by anonymous retail investors in Europe would be a public relations disaster, while the Japanese institutional investors would be somehow better able to "absorb" the shock, just as

Japanese commercial creditors are being forced to do. An additional consideration is the expectation of bilateral economic and financial support from Germany, and the desire to maintain a favorable image in the German financial community and with German retail investors.[12]

A Brief History of Sovereign Defaults[13]

It is worth analyzing the experience of sovereign bond debt restructurings and defaults at the beginning of this century as some interesting and instructive parallels can be drawn to the situation today. Capital markets have experienced large overseas defaults three times in the last hundred years, most recently in the 1920s and 1930s. The crisis began with only three countries in serious default in the 1920s (Mexico, Ecuador, and the Soviet Union) and spread worldwide in the following decade. Studies of historical international lending experience have concluded that there was no apparent relationship between the severity of interwar default and the ability to borrow immediately following World War II. Even more important, the studies show no evidence of any market tendency to discriminate among countries according to their debt service records in previous periods, in particular by "rationing in ... the faithful servicers." All portfolio lending remained depressed for decades as American and European investors concluded that foreign direct investment was preferable to bond purchases. Portfolio capital flows recovered only in the early 1970s, pushed by money-center banks. Until the inception of the international debt crisis in 1982, the international market for bank loans replaced the market for international bonds and foreign direct investment as the major source of private capital for development.

Defaults in 1931 on interest and amortization by every Latin American country except Argentina were followed by defaults in Southern and Eastern Europe. By 1933 the largest borrower of American funds, Germany, had defaulted on all foreign bond obligations. American investors purchased a disproportionate share of speculative bonds issued for foreign municipalities and corporations, while London specialized in new sovereign issues for the Commonwealth and colonies, and devoted a smaller share of capital than New York to riskier loans to Latin American and Central Europe. London's behavior may be attributable to a more experienced market, to long-standing political and financial ties to the Commonwealth, to preferential British tax treatment of colonial issues, or to the Bank of England's sporadic embargoes on foreign issues. The combined result of these factors was a significantly lower incidence of default on sterling than on dollar issues.

The Case of Brazil. Brazil illustrates negotiations in the 1930s era of bond finance. The decline in foreign exchange receipts due to the steady deterioration of the terms of trade throughout the 1920s, followed by the collapse of exports during the Depression, led the government in October 1931 to suspend interest payments on most of the nation's external debt.[14] Plans to issue 20- and 40-year funding bonds to capitalize interest arrears were announced the following year. But in 1934, on the advice of British financial experts, Brazil announced a plan to restructure the debt. The three-year Aranha Plan limited debt service to roughly half of Brazil's net export receipts. Bonds were divided into seven grades, with funding loans and other select obligations to receive full interest, other federal, state, and local obligations partial interest, and certain state and municipal loans no interest. At the end of three years, following little improvement in the situation, debt service payments were suspended again. Following sporadic negotiations with creditors, Brazil announced another temporary settlement in 1940 under which these seven categories of bonds were to receive interest at modified rates. Finally, in 1943 Brazil negotiated a permanent readjustment with bondholders. There is a striking resemblance to today's

---

12   cf. also the chapter on Hungary and Bulgaria in the International Bond Markets.

13   This section is entirely summarized from Eichengreen and Portes, Chapter 5, The Developing Country Debt Crisis, World Bank, 1989.

14   Coffee prices declined by 43 percent from 1929 to 1930 alone.

debt reduction negotiations in that creditors were offered a menu of options. These ranged from a plan that would reduce interest rates from 30% to 70% of contractual levels, to a plan in which they would surrender 20% to 50% of capital in exchange for a cash payment of 6% to 60% of par value and somewhat higher interest rates on the remainder. In particular, Brazil's proposal to issue 20- and 40-year funding bonds sounds like what bankers saw on the table in October 1990.

Portfolio Returns. Eichengreen and Portes have calculated the realized rates of return on overseas bonds issued in the 1920s. Their conclusion is that, for creditors with diversified portfolios who were willing to hold out for final settlement, the 1930s defaults were not disastrous. On average, British and American investors recovered their principal. The realized internal rate of return on a country average basis reached negative levels only in extreme cases (-7.4% for Brazil, -9.8% for Bolivia, and -14.8% for Hungary), where not just interest but substantial principal was written off. The average nominal internal rate of return (weighted by issue value) was roughly 4% on dollar bonds and 5% on sterling issues. Dollar bondholders settled for about half the contractual interest, and sterling bondholders settled for slightly more. However, dollar bondholders did only marginally worse than if they had held domestic Treasury bonds, and sterling bondholders did somewhat better. Ex-ante risk premiums nearly compensated American bondholders for foreign lending risks, and they compensated British bondholders in full.

2. MACROECONOMIC CONSIDERATIONS IN REESTABLISHING ACCESS TO CAPITAL MARKETS

A country's ability to work its way out of its debt problems and reestablish credibility with foreign lenders is essentially a macroeconomic issue. All creditworthiness indicators look for sustainable capacity to transfer resources abroad to meet debt service obligations. Specifically, persistent current account deficits accompanied by insufficient capital inflows to maintain adequate reserves—and the resulting accumulations of external obligations—usually indicate that debt service will soon be disrupted. In 1986, medium- and long-term public debt accounted for some three-quarters of total foreign debt in middle-income developing countries.[15]

An important role of foreign capital is to supplement domestic resources in accelerating capital formation. An essential feature of the successful examples of external debt accumulation is that the borrowing fueled capital accumulation and thus output growth. Faster growth reduces debt-output ratios over time, or at least slows their rate of increase. Two further criteria in determining the effectiveness of this process are (1) the availability of domestic savings and (2) the incremental capital output ratio (ICOR), the productivity of capital. The higher the marginal savings rate (proportion of incremented income saved and available for reinvestment), the greater the likelihood that the borrower can service foreign borrowings and simultaneously reduce the savings-investment gap. The higher the return on investment (the lower the ICOR), the greater the availability of resources for new investment and for servicing foreign borrowings. The savings-investment mechanism is at the center of this process, and the marginal and average savings rates are indexes of the country's capacity to mobilize its own resources for development, to service its borrowings and ultimately to reach the stage in which growth is self-financed.

At the same time, other things being equal, higher real interest rates on external debt increase indicators of indebtedness by accelerating the growth of debt service costs.[16] For any given transfer of principal plus interest payments, the debt-output ratio increases if real interest rates on past debt exceed the economy's real growth rate. Given the sharp rise in real interest rates in the 1980s, these now outstrip the real growth rates of most debtor economies, even those of fast-growth economies like Turkey. Furthermore, many debtors have financed payments on their external debt by issuing more expensive domestic debt. The increased interest burden resulting from such "debt swaps" raises the fiscal deficit and contributes to escalating domestic real interest rates.

The central question is how to bring about the necessary surplus of domestic savings over investment at levels of investment high enough to sustain output growth. An important element is the extent to which the public sector contributes directly to the necessary improvement in the savings surplus. The fiscal deficit will typically need to be brought down. Public borrowing requirements affect the current account deficit, the inflation rate (or at least expectations of inflation), the growth of the domestic and external debt, and eventually the level of economic activity. Thus the country usually needs sustained and extensive fiscal adjustment to generate the internal resources in the public sector in order to meet its debt service obligations. But, if the fiscal cutbacks are assumed to come from public investment as well as consumption, there could be unintended results. Private investment may well be "crowded in" as a result of lower real interest rates following the shrinkage of public sector borrowing. The cut in public

---

15 That is the debt guaranteed by or owed by the sovereign. The rest was debt owed abroad by private entities in the developing country with no guarantee. Banks have tried to include this in their rescheduling agreements, with mixed success.

16 Van Wijnbergen, External Debt, Inflation and the Public Sector: Toward Fiscal Policy for Sustainable Growth, in The World Bank Economic Review, September 1989.

investment could, however, more than offset this increase in private investment. This will reduce output growth, which in turn reduces the private sector's savings surplus. Van Wijnbergen concludes that, in a growth-oriented adjustment program, high real interest rates may be necessary to make sure that a large enough private savings surplus is generated to achieve consistency in fiscal deficits and targets for external balance. To make sure that most of the effect of the high real rates is shifted toward consumption rather than investment, a government can use investment incentives and tax measures to deflect the impact of high real interest rates away from investment.

If foreign borrowings are undertaken, the key question is whether future export earnings can service such debt. External debt is managed more easily if the borrowings are at least in part related to investment programs that will enhance export earnings. If so, countries can even experience current account deficits for an initial period without adversely affecting their creditworthiness, provided that the deficits reflect investments that strengthen the country's external position and the shortfalls are financed with sufficiently long-term capital. For example, South Korea's economic development strategy emphasizing heavy investment in export capacity led to current account deficits averaging 5.6% of GDP from 1974-81. This period was followed by rapid export growth and increasing current account surpluses that reached 8.3% of GDP by 1988, sufficiently large to permit even prepayment of external debt during 1986-88.

A country's capacity for external borrowing involves two considerations: solvency and creditworthiness. Solvency concerns ability to pay and is linked to the non-interest current account (national income minus consumption minus interest expenditure), to the real rates of interest and output growth, and the initial debt. Clearly, the lower the debt stock, the higher the level of sustainable borrowings. Second, the more expensive a country's external debt, the higher the surplus needed on the non-interest current account to maintain solvency. Third, the higher a country's growth rate, the more leeway it has in borrowing without jeopardizing solvency. To remain solvent, a country should not plan expenditures higher in discounted value terms than its current (and discounted) future income, minus its initial debt.[17]

Creditworthiness refers to the lender's assessment of the borrower's ability as well as willingness to repay. Repayment requires not only a high enough value of resources to repay but also a surplus of traded goods production over traded goods consumption (net exports). Generating this surplus is likely to be more difficult for a country that has most of its goods in nontraded sectors. As a result, this country may be more tempted not to repay, even if it is solvent. That is why debt-export (or debt-service to export) ratios are a useful proxy in assessing creditworthiness.[18]

---

17 In equilibrium, the current discounted value of income minus expenditure is $(Y-C-I)/(r^*-n)$. r^* is the average real interest rate on foreign debt, n the real growth rate of the economy and b^* is the share of initial debt stock in output. For the non-interest current account surplus not to fall short of the initial debt, the following must hold: $NICA > (r^*-n) b^*$. This implies that the NICA should on average equal at least the initial debt times the difference between the real interest cost of foreign debt and the real output growth rate.

18 An annex we have listed the debt ratio statistics of ten countries from Latin America, Eastern Europe and Asia - i.e. those countries we are referring to in the study, analyzing ratios of total debt to GNP, interest to GNP, the amount of total debt to the countries' exports and, last, the debt service to exports, a ratio commonly referred to as the debt service ratio. These ten countries' ratios are then compared to the average ratios of severely indebted middle income countries and moderately indebted middle income countries. Ratios are given both for the year 1984 and 1989.

3. RECENT CONVERSION BONDS

In 1988 and 1989, Finance Minister Miyazawa of Japan, President Mitterrand of France, and Treasury Secretary Brady of the United States made proposals to include debt and debt service reductions more formally in debt strategy and to promote some form of official support for such transactions. The basic idea was to reduce the debt overhang for those countries that (1) followed a medium-term macroeconomic adjustment program, (2) had a viable medium-term external financing plan consistent with the adjustment program which would be facilitated by debt and debt service reductions, and (3) had reasonable prospects that the additional resources would enhance growth and development prospects, primarily by increasing investments. These Brady-type debt restructurings—and their direct implications for the countries involved—have been discussed in great detail in other publications.[19] In this section we will focus on the principal implications such transactions have on the bond markets since, literally overnight, billions of dollars of commercial bank loans have been transformed into bonds.

Characteristics

We now look at the bond structures resulting from the recent conversions in Mexico and Venezuela. Although the Venezuelan bonds basically follow the structure of the Mexican bonds, which were restructured earlier, some distinct characteristics are worth noting.

A basic characteristic of the restructuring is that the banks holding the debt exchange their existing loans for bonds. For Mexico, the banks could choose between interest reduction bonds with a fixed coupon of 6.25% on 100% of the face value of the old debt, and principal reduction bonds for the face value of 65% of the original debt, on which six-month Libor plus a spread of 13/16% would be paid. Both bonds have a 30-year maturity and principal collateralized by a US Treasury zero coupon bond with matching maturity. These bonds carry rolling interest collateral equivalent to 12 to 18 months interest. The bonds are in registered form. Bonds with a total face value of US$35.5 billion were created instantly; US$35.5 billion worth of bonds were thus added to the international bond markets.[20]

For Venezuela, loans were restructured in a similar way, except that Venezuela provides 14 months of rolling interest collateral. The principal reduction bonds have a discount of only 30%, and the fixed coupon is set at 6.75%. In addition, banks could opt for a new money structure, a buyback, or temporary interest reduction bonds, which pay a fixed coupon of 5% for the first two years, 6% for the following two years and 7% in year five. After that, the bonds pay 7/8% over Libor. There was no discount and only the reduced interest payments were collateralized—that is, only up to and including year five. These latter bonds are in bearer form.[21] A total of US$19.5 billion was transformed into bonds, including new money bonds for Venezuela. A detailed description of the transactions can be found in the annex on debt and debt service reduction packages.

In a slightly different category are those new issues linked to new money provisions in Brady-type debt reductions: new money bonds. This option has appeared in the financing packages on Mexico, Philippines, Venezuela, and Uruguay. Costa Rica explicitly rejected any request for new money, and it is also widely believed that Costa Rica does not expect to return to commercial markets anytime soon. The new money bonds that have been linked to Brady deals, all uncollateralized, are shown below.

---

19   For instance: Ruben Lamdany, Voluntary debt reduction operations: Bolivia, Mexico and Beyond, World Bank Discussion Paper No 52.

20   About $12 billion of discount bonds, $23 billion of par and $500 million of "new money" bonds.

21   See Salomon Brothers, Evaluating the Venezuela 1990 financing plan. July 1990.

Table 1-New Money Bonds Linked to Brady Operations   (US$ million)

Issuer	Amount of New Money Bonds	Total Volume of Brady Bonds	Interest on New Money Bonds	Maturity/Grace
Mexico	500	35,000	Libor + 13/16%	15/7
Philippines	700	None	Libor + 13/16%	15/8
Venezuela	1,200	19,000	Libor + 1%	15/7
Uruguay	90	535	Libor + 1%	15/7

Creditors who did not wish to reduce the face value of their outstanding claims on Mexico could choose to reschedule eligible debt for 16 years with four years of grace and, in addition, purchase new money bonds equal to 25% of their exposure over four years without enhancement. All the 1990 financing plan bonds, including the new money bonds, received special rights to debt equity conversions. (A smaller amount of new money, US$500 million, was provided in this way than had been anticipated).

Creditors of Venezuela wishing to protect the face value of their exposure could select debt conversion bonds (17 years, seven years grace, Libor+7/8%), with the provision that they purchase new money bonds equal to 20% of the amount of debt converted. The Venezuelan new money bonds were to be issued in two series, by the Republic of Venezuela and the Central Bank respectively, and would pay 1% and 7/8% over Libor. Both series were to have a final maturity of 15 years, with seven years' grace, issued in three tranches through 1992. The new money bonds would be issued in bearer form, with no collateralization of principal or interest. It was estimated that US$6 billion of debt would be allocated to the debt conversion option and therefore US$1.2 billion of new money bonds would be issued.

Chile recently adopted a novel approach to issuing a Eurobond. It has insisted on including a US$320 million Eurobond in its US$4.5 billion commercial-bank debt refinancing package. The maturity is five years, with a three-year amortization, and the coupon is 1.5% over Libor. As of December 15, 1990 the bond was about 80% subscribed by banks. Basically this bond will be held by banks participating in the country's refinancing transaction. It is expected that more bonds will be issued soon, targeted at retail and institutional investors.

Implications

These conversions have direct implications for the bond markets, since the debt no longer falls under the category of "loans" but is now trading as bonds. As long as these new bonds continue to be held by the banking community, which held the loans prior to the conversions, no real addition is made to the international bond markets. Recently, however, these bonds have been sold both to institutions and to private high-net-worth investors who want to increase the return on their portfolios.[22]

The restructuring of the Mexican debt (and, for that matter, of the Venezuelan debt) has been done on the assumption that the bonds will not be subject to further debt rescheduling or

---

22   In some cases the Brady bonds have been sold on margins, i.e., Banks have been willing to accept the Brady bonds as collateral on loans (to buy the bonds).

restructuring. As the bonds have a 30-year maturity, the chance that these bonds might not be serviced punctually over their whole life cannot be excluded. In that case, the investors holding the debt would bear the losses which, up to now, have been assumed by the banks.

An additional complication, in the case of the Venezuelan temporary interest reduction bonds, is that these bonds will be in bearer form. This implies that they will be perceived to have seniority status similar to the Venezuelan Eurobonds.

If the principal collateral provided by the US Treasury is "stripped away," so that only the interest cash flows that Mexico and Venezuela must pay are calculated, the Mexican and Venezuelan conversions prove to be a bigger risk for investors than recent Mexican or Venezuelan Euroissues.

Brady bonds are trading according to different criteria. Their price movement is determined basically by supply and demand from the commercial banks which, again, is frequently established not by fundamental market factors but by balance sheet and accounting factors. Thus prices are likely to be depressed in September because Canadian banks are selling before the end of their fiscal year, and in November, when the US banks are selling before their end of year.[23] This has the added implication that investors would not participate to the same extent if there were a major rally in Mexican bonds, and also that they are likely to be hit whenever the holders of the bonds (the banks) have to undertake balance sheet restructurings. Similarly, one would intuitively expect the value of Mexican Brady bonds to have increased at the time of the oil price rise in early August 1990 due to the invasion of Kuwait. In fact, the secondary market price of Mexican bonds fell, because a large number of Middle East banks reportedly decided to sell their holdings of such bonds to improve their liquidity.

If the Brady bonds become subject to another round of debt restructuring—and if private investors are therefore hit—it is feared that the fragile confidence of investors in new Mexican and Venezuelan issues would be destroyed as a result of confusion over the two types of bonds. The Euromarkets could then be closed to Mexican and Venezuelan borrowers for a long time. In this context it is difficult to predict whether private borrowers would also be cut off from the bond markets. Judging from the period during the 1980s, when neither public nor private borrowers could tap the international bond markets, it is doubtful whether investors would continue buying new issues of private corporates in the Eurobond or the US domestic markets if Mexico or Venezuela are unable to service their Brady bonds punctually. It is not clear whether this hypothetical effect would be carried over to private borrowers, since they can pledge specific assets and the legal recourse of bondholders is better defined. Given the uncertainties of proceeding with legal action against sovereigns, it appears that private sector borrowers are more attractive to investors ex ante. Investors would still need, however, to be aware of developments in sovereign debt repayment performance, since this would likely have repercussions on private borrowers' access to foreign exchange for debt service purposes.

---

23 1990 saw a revision of the trend as commercial banks could not set off their developing country assets due to problems with other credits.

4. MEXICO'S REENTRY TO THE INTERNATIONAL BOND MARKETS[24]

For a highly indebted country which has recently undergone a commercial debt workout involving substantial losses for its creditors, the crucial question is how to make the transition back to the world of private voluntary lending. As mentioned earlier, most countries have fully serviced their outstanding bond obligations throughout periods of economic difficulty. This performance record makes bonds a natural vehicle for a country seeking to reenter the capital markets. The country must be certain, however, that "new issue bonds" are kept separate in the minds of investors from the often large volume of Brady bonds. Mexico has been particularly successful in tapping the markets for new issues very shortly after its debt restructuring. We analyze the Mexican approach in detail here, and in later sections offer comparisons with other selected sovereign issuers.

Mexico's eight-year exile from the international capital markets is over. In the past year, Mexican companies, both public and private, have raised more than US$500 million through a wide range of instruments, including specially structured securitized bonds, conventional high-yield issues as well as convertibles. Equally remarkable is the fact that both institutional investors and high net worth individuals, including nationals using their US dollar assets abroad, are taking a major share of the bond issues.

During the greater part of the 1980s, Mexican securities were considered "exotic," reserved for investors willing to accept high risk for a high return. Mexican borrowers have, however, maintained an impeccable record in the securities market for interest and principal payments. Two examples will illustrate this claim. At the time of the 1980s crises, Pemex, the state-owned oil company, had a number of Eurobonds outstanding in several currencies. Among the largest was a US$125 million floating rate note, issued in March 1981 at a rate of 1/4% over six-month Libor for an original term of 10 years. The issue contained a holders' put option (to require payment of principal on October 8, 1988). This option was exercised, and the issue was repaid in full. In a similar case, Telmex, the state-owned telephone company, had issued US$75 million in floating rate notes in June 1981 with an original term of 10 years, again at a rate of 1/4% over six-month Libor. This issue also contained the early repayment option, exercised by the holders on December 23, 1988. Mexican commercial banks, nationalized in 1982, have an equally solid record for repayment of securities issues.

In the analysis that follows, we highlight the most important events and provide some background information. Because our focus is on deals that are exceptional in some respect, not all new deals are discussed in detail. A complete list of recent capital market transactions is in the table at the end.

Chronology of Events

Between the late 1970s and 1982, Mexico rapidly increased its external bond issues, as domestic entities turned to global capital markets to supplement syndicated loans from private commercial banks. The annual volume averaged US$908 million during 1975-82, and peaked in 1981, when US$2.2 billion of new securities were placed in the international markets. Since August 1982, however, when the government was temporarily unable to meet its current obligations to commercial bank creditors, Mexico's access to international capital markets had been suspended. Except for two private placements by Mexican commercial banks, Somex and Banco Internacional in 1986, Mexico had not entered the markets in recent years. In fact, the two 1986

---

24 Information in this section of the paper was compiled from discussions with market participants. Details on the structures of specific deals come from the May and June 1990 issues of Latin Finance magazine and selected issues of the International Financing Review.

private placements resulted from a conversion of existing interbank lines into medium-term notes, arranged by First Interstate Bank.

Securitizations. The first new issues were securitized in the form of private placements. Securitization is a technique by which future earnings of a company are bought on a net present value basis, often in the form of receivables, and are used as collateral, guaranteeing the payments for the bonds which are issued to raise the money for the purchase of the security. Car loans, mortgages, or credit card receivables can be taken off a bank's balance sheet by an upfront purchase. Similarly, once Telmex can establish that it will have a receivables overhang from AT&T,[25] Telmex can sell these receivables to an investor, who would give Telmex cash upfront for the purchase. Likewise, the electricity exporter Comision Federal de Electricidad (CFE) could sell electricity receivables and get cash upfront from investors who were willing to accept the risk. In effect, by using receivables, companies can circumvent the problem of credit risk by shifting it to a great extent outside the country. This arrangement has been used in several Latin American countries.

Since 1987 Telmex has issued three five-year private placements for a total of US$900 million, backed by AT&T receivables and arranged by Citicorp. Although the real risk for investors in these transactions was AT&T and not Telmex, the deals reintroduced a Mexican name into the market and thus drew analysts' attention back to the country. Citicorp arranged two further transactions for Banamex (US$130 million, three years) and Bancomer (US$230 million, five years), which it placed with US and other foreign institutional investors. Securitized credit card receivables served as collateral in both these issues.

Salomon Brothers placed a US$235 million, five-year bond for the Comision Federal de Electricidad (CFE) with five institutional investors, including one insurance company that is reported to have bought half of the bonds. Although the risk was shifted from CFE to the receivables from US purchasers of Mexican electricity, which collateralized the deal, a yield as high as 11.5% was still perceived to be necessary.

Bond Issues. In June 1989 Merrill Lynch engineered Latin America's first unsecured public sector Eurobond since the 1982 debt crisis: a US$100 million issue for Bancomext (BNCE), the development bank for trade finance. The bonds carried a fixed coupon of 10 1/4% payable quarterly and were not collateralized. Principal was to be repaid in 20 equal quarterly installments through June 15, 1994, which shortened the average life of the issue to 2.5 years. (BNCE made the first payment on these notes—US$5 million of principal and US$2.6 million of interest—on September 15, 1989.) The launch yield of the bonds was about 17%.

The transaction was criticized for the pricing of the issue. A yield of 17% seems very high now, especially in view of the fact that it subsequently traded down to around 12%. The fact remains, however, that the deal was launched amid the Mexican rescheduling negotiations with commercial banks, without collateral, and with no benchmark. It is only on the foundation of this initial issue that subsequent borrowers could get better terms.

During the following year, Mexico's largest export-oriented companies took advantage of the windows in the markets to raise money abroad, tapping both the Euromarkets (in

---

25 Telmex has a revenue-sharing arrangement with AT&T whereby calls to Mexico that originate in the US must pay Telmex for use of the Mexican network and vice versa. Because of the imbalance in telephone traffic, Telmex has a regular stream of dollar receivables from AT&T. Similarly, CFE regularly sells its surplus electricity to US public utilities across the border, and was able to pledge these receivables to securitize its first five-year bond issue.

DM, US$, and Austrian Schillings (ASCH)[26] as well as the US domestic private placement/Rule 144a market.

As an example of the latter, J.P. Morgan placed a US$100 million bond in the newly opened Rule 144a domestic US market for Telmex with a number of institutional investors.[27]

The 1990 Cemex issue represents another Latin American first: convertible bonds.[28] Investors in the Cemex convertibles will be able to convert 51.97% of each semiannual coupon payment into shares of Cemex-controlled Tolteca Mexicana (Tolmex) common stock represented by American depository receipts (ADRs). Further, 64.3% of the principal amount may be converted into Tolmex ADRs. The initial three-year bond issue can be renewed four times, with increasing amounts of principal and interest payments eligible for conversion into Tolmex stock. The interest rate on the bonds rises to 14% annually following the first renewal.[29]

The conversion option in this deal is so far out of the money that it did not influence the pricing (reduce the yield) of the issue. The International Finance Corporation did not participate in this transaction for exactly that reason.

Another interesting example of the broadening of the market for Mexican borrowers is the US$65 million Eurobond issue for La Moderna, a Monterrey cigarette company almost entirely dependent on domestic sales and thus with no US dollar income to service debt.[30] The issue reintroduced to the Euromarkets a totally domestic Mexican company that would have to service its debt from its domestic cash flows. The bonds had a tenor of 2.5 years, carried an intial yield of over 16%, and were placed among 25 different buyers, according to Bear Stearns, the lead manager.[31] The borrower's impeccable credit record facilitated this issue. The company had issued unsecured international debt in 1981, consisting of a US$20 million loan syndicated to a group of banks, including several international banks, and a US$30 million Eurobond. Both transactions were serviced as scheduled, despite the difficult conditions in Mexico at the time.

The state-owned development bank Nafinsa[32] recently completed a US$100 million financing with a five-year bullet maturity, an 11 3/4% coupon (payable semiannually), and a pricc of 98.75% to yield 12.45%. The issue was oversubscribed and trading at a premium shortly after it was launched, a reflection in part of Nafinsa's creditworthiness. The issue, which has become the pricing benchmark for similar borrowings, includes a put option for the investor after three years, at a strike price of 98.45%. The management group included numerous US, European, and Japanese banks.

The pricing of this deal was made easier by the success of the previous DM issue for Nafinsa, which Dresdner Bank had brought to the market. That five-year deal carried a coupon of 11% and yielded over 11.50% (after fees) at the time of the launch. Most of the paper was placed with German retail customers and with high-net-worth individuals in Latin America.

---

26 Rule 144a is described in the section on Investor Profiles.

27 The bonds are senior and unsecured.

28 Cemex's decision to sell a portion of its 85% control of another company to lower its financing costs is unprecedented in Latin America.

29 Latin Finance, June 1990.

30 The investor had to accept the risk that La Moderna might not be able to convert its domestic revenues into US dollars for the interest payments.

31 Latin Finance, June 1990.

32 Nafinsa has full faith and credit of the United Mexican States.

Pemex is another successful Mexican Eurobond issuer. Having launched a DM 100 million transaction in Germany in early 1990, the company came to the Austrian capital market in July. Its six-year ASCH500 million issue met with considerable interest from retail and institutional investors from Germany, Switzerland, the Middle East and Far East as well as Austria. The 11% coupon is payable annually, and with its six-year bullet maturity, the issue is the longest deal currently in the market. On the basis of its par issue price, the deal was launched at a 240 basis point spread over the government benchmark issues.

Based on the success of Pemex in the Euromarkets, Paine Webber completed a US$100 million five-year deal for the borrower in the US domestic market with a yield of 11.43%, giving institutional investors a return of some 300 basis points over Treasuries.[33]

Based on the success of that issue, Pemex in September 1990 came to the Eurodollar market with a US$150 million three-year issue (11.625% coupon, issue price: 99.70%), lead-managed by the Swiss Bank Corp. In late 1988, Operadora de Bolsa arranged a $52 million private placement for Grupo Sanluis. The bond had a two-year maturity and carried a launch-yield of 16%.

Swaps. There generally is little information available about the extent to which Mexican borrowers swapped foreign currency proceeds into US dollar obligations. The ASCH issue apparently remained unswapped, whereas some issues by Mexican public sector borrowers have been swapped into US$ Libor issues. The general problem with cross currency swaps is the high risk for a counterpart when it books the transaction with Mexico. In the event of default, the swap would have to be replaced by a new transaction in the market, at a potentially great loss.

Euro CDs. Foreign branches of Mexican commercial banks in London and New York have been issuing CDs with maturities of up to six months. This market started about a year ago with relatively high yields as an arbitrage between the very high domestic dollar borrowing costs and the relatively cheaper dollar funds that could be obtained abroad. Even at the beginning of 1990, six-month CDs were still yielding over 15%. Many banks--and corporations through banks--tapped this market. Initially there was the additional advantage that funds borrowed by corporations in this manner were not subject to Mexico's withholding tax. Recently, however, lower domestic interest rates, the imposition of a withholding tax, and increased competition, lowered yields to about 12.75% - 13.00% in August 1990. The total volume of CDs issued is estimated at US$500 million for the first six months of 1990.

Special Reasons for Mexican Bond Investments

The new issues launched for Mexico in 1989-90 took place in the following context. Mexico has implemented major policy reforms to allow its economy to develop steadily. For a variety of reasons, the country is seen to be moving out of the Third World category, and gradually into the "investor grade" class. In the US, Europe, and Latin America—and to some extent, in the Middle East—Far East investors are starting to look at Mexican debt again. Mexico is perceived to have mastered the problems of the 1980s. At first, the chance of hefty capital gains due to a tightening of yields was also a major factor in the new issues. Certain institutions are also looking at sovereign high-yield debt as a replacement for their corporate junk-bonds after that sector collapsed in the US. The fact that, with higher oil prices, the Mexican economy will strengthen even further will certainly attract more institutional investors and might turn short-term (capital gain) investors into longer-term bond holders, adding stability to the market.

---

33 Although this deal was done as a private placement, it could qualify as a bond under Rule 144a.

In July 1986 Mexican authorities adopted a stabilization program, supported by the international financial institutions and commercial creditors, which included major policy changes designed to integrate Mexico more fully with the world economy. Mexico joined GATT (the General Agreement on Tariffs and Trade) that year and initiated a fast and far-reaching trade liberalization. Exchange rate policies were also made more favorable to all tradable sectors. Partly in response to a sharp nominal devaluation, inflation accelerated into triple digits (160%) by the end of 1987. The government responded by negotiating an Economic Solidarity Pact (Pacto) with labor, business and agricultural sector representatives to freeze minimum wages, public sector prices and tariffs, and the nominal exchange rate against the US dollar. Fiscal and monetary policy were further tightened, and structural reform efforts were intensified in the form of continued trade liberalization, divestiture of public sector assets, deregulation, and reform of industrial policy to encourage competition. The Pacto, originally intended for only a few months, has been renewed at intervals, and a new Pacto known as the Stabilization and Growth Pact (PECE) is still in effect. Under the PECE, public sector prices and tariffs were adjusted, minimum wages increased by 8%, and the peso/dollar exchange rate depreciated daily by one peso. Inflation declined to 52% in 1988 and to about 20% in 1989.

The new administration of President Salinas de Gortari, which took office in December 1988, has pledged to complement economic reforms with increased political openness and democratization as part of a general strategy of modernization. Sensitive sectors, such as trucking and petroleum, have seen substantial deregulation and the departure of certain well-established, influential labor leaders. There have been sweeping policy changes on the domestic front and on the external front, often going beyond the targets originally agreed to with multilateral lenders. A reorientation of incentives to eliminate the antiexport bias resulted in manufacturing sector export revenues surpassing oil export revenues in 1989. Manufacturing export revenues have quadrupled in the last two and a half years.

In addition to the impressive macroeconomic adjustment and trade reforms by the Mexican economy in 1985-88, Mexican issuers had several advantages over other developing country issuers in the international capital markets. The 2,000-mile frontier with the United States provided important familiarity and proximity benefits, in addition to housing a growing "maquiladora" (in-bond assembly) industry owned predominantly by US businesses. Mexico's oil reserves also predisposed investors to regard Mexico as lower risk. Most important, recent public discussions of a soon to be concluded free trade zone encompassing Mexico and the United States have effectively put Mexico in a different category from other developing country bond issuers despite Mexico's recent dramatic difficulties in servicing commercial debt.

The successful conclusion of Mexico's negotiations with its commercial creditors toward a Brady Plan and the proposal to extend its privatization program to the domestic banking sector have contributed greatly to improving the confidence of foreign investors in the economy. Predictions are for the GDP to grow by about 4.5% annually, following zero real growth and a severe decline in per capita income between 1982 and 1988. The recent oil price increase should also provide a favorable boost to the current and fiscal accounts. The estimated oil price for the 1990 government budget was US$13 per barrel.

Summary for Mexico

Developments during the last two years have shown that the appetite for Mexican debt was not an isolated occurrence. On the contrary, there seems to be steady demand for Mexican paper on a high yield, unsecured basis, for maturities up to five years. As more Mexican bonds launched in the late 1970s and early 1980s mature, and investors seek to replace them, this demand is likely to be strengthened.

Still, the main reason for the success of Mexican issues in the markets has been Mexico's economic performance. Only on this basis and only by adhering strictly to certain borrowing criteria will Mexico be able to tap the markets consistently in the future.

Even though the Mexican government has only recently finished restructuring its debt, with major losses for the participating commercial banks, the "United Mexican States" have already become a successful issuer in the markets, pursued by numerous prime investment banks. The first sovereign bond since the debt crisis was issued in February 1991, in the amount of DM 300 million with a maturity of five years and a launch yield of 10.37%.

According to a number of market sources[34], traded financial instruments such as Eurobonds, covertibles and Rule 144a private placements have begun to replace traditional commercial bank loans as Mexico's strong performance attracts new foreign capital. State companies such as PEMEX, Nafin, BNCE as well as Cemex, a private company, dominate the US dollar bond market both in terms of absolute number and dollar value. The consensus is that there is demand among investors for at least US$500 million in new issues annually, since this is the volume of principal on outstanding bonds that Mexico retires, and investors look to replenish their portfolios. Recently, however, demand for such issues exceeded supply. In addition, over US$2 billion in foreign direct investment in Mexico was recorded in 1990.

The average maturity of Mexican issues has increased from 3.2 years in 1990 to 3.8 years in 1991. At the same time it should be noted that five of the seven issues with maturities after 1994 are puttable before 1994. Issuers, especially sovereign agencies, have incorporated put options to address the concerns of investors about maturities extending beyond the current presidential administration. While most Mexican medium term bonds are denominated in US dollars, the Government and its agencies have also issued in DM, ECU and Austrian Schillings. Traders report that issues which trade most frequently (are most liquid) have the following characteristics: i) they are issued more recently; ii) they are large (US$100 million and above); and iii) they are Eurobonds rather than private placements.

Most of the issues placed since 1989 have had bullet amortization structures--while most Eurobonds pay annual coupons, however, Mexican medium term issues pay coupons quarterly, semiannually and annually. The yields track US Treasury securities, suggesting that investors assess the risk-return profile as a spread over Treasuries. Nafin, for instance, has issued two five year bonds in the past twelve months. The first issue, in August 1990, was priced at 398 basis points over the relevant Treasury, while the May 1991 issue came at 210 basis points over, reflecting investors' perceptions that risk has declined.

---

34 These findings are reported in the July 23, 1991 issue of JP Morgan's newsletter from the Developing Country Asset Trading Desk.

5. TURKEY'S REENTRY TO THE CAPITAL MARKETS

The international financial institutions were the main providers of capital to Turkey in the early 1980s, and little or no additional medium- and long-term funding could be obtained for nonproject purposes.[35] Turkey became once again active in the syndicated bank loan market in 1984, when confidence was restored in the government's ability to adjust its economy successfully. Most of the syndications were for project financing; the only ones for balance-of-payments support were those linked with IBRD adjustment loans. It appears that World Bank support was catalytic. Starting in 1985, Turkey began approaching the Japanese market to augment World Bank loans for various sector adjustment efforts. All of them involved syndicates of Japanese commercial banks and life insurance institutions that supported Turkey's requests for balance of payments financing. The syndicated Eurodollar loan market, by contrast, was mainly interested in project finance and was reserving its position for participation in large build-operate-transfer (BOT) projects, such as highways, a metrorail, and a thermal power plant construction. The stratification—with Japan providing BOP funds and the European markets supplying project finance—suited Turkey's interest and lenders' interests.

Turkey has had a presence in the German capital markets for some time. The Dresdner Scheme is a special arrangement between Dresdner Bank and the Central Bank of Turkey to attract the foreign currency deposits of Turkish workers residing in Germany. About 90% of the deposits are in DM. The Central Bank of Turkey sets the interest rates offered under the scheme—slightly higher than normal deposit rates—and Dresdner Bank acts only as the agent to facilitate the remittances to Turkey, so that depositors have Turkish risk. The scheme has turned out to be a significant source of funding for Turkey, and this funding has continued to increase while the volume of borrowings from other sources declined.[36]

Beginning in 1987 there was a shift in strategy, when Turkey found financing opportunities in Europe through the German bond market. Between February 1987 and July 1989, Turkey issued seven bonds in the German capital market, ranging from DM125 million to DM500 million, for a total of DM2,025 million (over US$1 billion). These funds have played a crucial role in helping Turkey meet its immediate debt service obligations. Moreover, the proceeds from the bond issues provided funds not otherwise available in the European syndicated loan market, given the banks' preference for project-linked finance. The decline in the spread over German government bonds (Bunds) [37] paid by Turkey appears due mainly to increased familiarity with "Turkish risk" despite the deterioration in Turkey's domestic indicators (rising inflation). But, a comparison of interest rates, spreads and maturities for Turkey in 1987 and 1988 shows that market terms improved slightly. This result is counterintuitive if one considers that Turkey's inflation rate rose from 50% to 75% from December 1987 to mid-1989. The market appears to give more weight to the improved image created by a strengthened current account in terms of access to international capital markets. Longer term, however, it is unlikely that the market will continue to ignore domestic economic imbalances.

Also in December 1988, Turkey entered the Eurodollar market for the first time in several years, with a Eurobond of US$150 million lead managed by Bankers Trust. In 1989

---

35 This information is taken from a World Bank Country Study titled Turkey--A Strategy for Managing Debt, Borrowings and Transfers Under Macroeconomic Adjustment. The Report is based on the findings of two Bank missions that visited Turkey in December 1988 and September 1989.

36 Turkey, p.29.

37 The first two issues were floated by the Central Bank of Turkey, and the spread paid over Bunds were relatively high at 210-160 basis points. The spread has declined with the subsequent five issues from 122 basis points to 92 basis points. The amounts raised through each issue rose to DM 300-500 million. While spreads have fallen, yields have increased from 7.09 to 7.90 percent, reflecting movements in interest rates in the German capital markets.

Turkey tapped the US$ Eurobond market four more times, for a total of US$750 million. Turkey had refrained from taking on US dollar borrowings from commercial sources for several years, except in the case of projects. This was due partly to high US interest rates and partly to the lack of interest among US banks for nonproject lending.

The first two bonds issued in 1989 were US$200 million each and show lengthened maturities (to 10 years). Since investors may exercise a put option at their discretion after five years, it is not clear what the effective maturity will be. Turkey has requested a credit rating from Standard and Poor's, which should improve its access to international capital markets by broadening the investor base.

The Turkish approach, therefore, was to begin by tapping into a market where it already had substantial connections and could be fairly sure of attracting Turkish nationals among its retail investors. (This is significant because it reduces the problem of investor acceptance for a first-time bond issuer). In a sense, Turkey was forced to turn to bond issues in the capital markets to obtain general purpose balance of payments funding—partly to refinance its existing commercial obligations—because banks exhibited a clear preference for project-linked finance. Having established a presence in the DM market, Turkey then turned to the Eurodollar market.

6. HUNGARY AND BULGARIA IN THE INTERNATIONAL CAPITAL MARKETS

Hungary and Bulgaria managed to tap the international bond markets in the 1980s. Hungary placed a large number of issues with great success, reflecting its special status among Eastern Bloc countries. Although experiencing a severe liquidity crisis in 1981-82, it had managed to improve its debt profile by shifting out from short-term to long-term debt. Hungary's debt grew rapidly from about US$8.8 billion in 1984 to over US$20 billion at the end of 1990, due mainly to current account deficits and fluctuations in cross exchange rates. Debt service ratios parallelled the rise in debt and by the spring of 1990, the country was close to a liquidity crisis.

The Hungarian authorities managed, however, to restore confidence by assuring the markets that they would not seek to restructure the debt or undertake Brady-type debt or debt-service reductions. The authorities maintained that, even after the elections and the transition from communism to a free market economy, the country could honor all existing debt obligations. Hungary also initiated a macroeconomic adjustment program, backed by the IMF. The World Bank helped the country in a US$200 million, 10-year Eurobond where, under a new arrangement, it guaranteed the principal repayment at maturity.[38] Participants perceived this to be a success as it restored confidence and enabled the National Bank of Hungary to tap the DM and ASCH market on its own. Although liquidity problems remain, Hungary is perceived as being in position to tap the markets now and in the future.

Bulgaria managed to tap the markets, but not as often or successfully as Hungary. On a smaller scale, it obtained relatively long-term, seven-year funds through a DM200 million Eurobond in June 1989. Unlike Hungary, Bulgaria had no history of liquidity problems. In fact, under the previous regime, Bulgaria was considered one of the most reliable East European borrowers. This may explain the relatively favorable terms it was able to obtain on its DM issue in June 1989, just five months before the change in government. (There was also a Japanese private placement of Y5 billion and a seven-year maturity for the Mineral Bank of Bulgaria).

With very few exceptions, foreign borrowings were centralized under the previous regime. Dealings with foreign creditors had always been very mechanical, with the Council of Ministers deciding on annual borrowing targets and a separate institution routinely conducting the borrowing. Foreign exchange reserves were maintained at comfortable levels of several months' import cover.

With the change of leadership in late 1989 and various institutional reforms that created uncertainties with regard to the law, commercial creditors began to retreat and Bulgaria was unable to refinance its existing debt. All amortization payments on its commercial obligations in the first quarter of 1990 were made from reserves. By the end of the second quarter, reserves had been reduced to a few days' import cover, and panic set in. In a remarkable development, authorities at the centralized foreign borrowing institution informed creditors—without advising any other part of the government—that it was suspending all debt service because of liquidity problems. The central bankers' inexperience in the financial market led them to believe this was an internal matter between themselves and their creditors, and there would be little or no repercussions.

Bulgaria's standing in international capital markets plummeted overnight, and has not since recovered. At the time, Bulgaria was not a member of the IBRD or the IMF, trade patterns with the Soviet Union (its largest trading partner) were shifting, and substantial receivables from both East Germany and Iraq were not being honored. In hindsight, it is noteworthy that as late as June 1989 Bulgaria had obtained access to the bond market despite rather

---

38 The principal of the issue was guaranteed under the World Bank's Expanded Cofinancing Operations (ECO) Program.

weak economic fundamentals and the absence of any well-defined strategy. Once the boat was rocked, all illusions about its creditworthiness were shattered. Bulgaria is now acknowledged to be insolvent, and it has been unable to service its commercial debt since March 1990. Until there is some resolution to the debt problem, its access to commercial credits is highly doubtful. As mentioned earlier, the only foreign obligation that has been honored since the moratorium is the interest payment on the DM bond, which was made on time in June 1990, and January and June 1991.

7. INVESTOR PROFILES

There is not one distinct type of investor but rather a wide variety of individuals and institutions who buy developing country paper for different reasons. Accordingly, we divide the analysis into regional markets—the US market, the Eurobond market, and the Samurai and yen private placement market. While the Eurobond market is probably the biggest market for developing country borrowers at present, the US capital markets are the largest in the world, measured by the volume of outstanding bond issues as well as annual gross funds raised. For this reason, they could prove, long term, to be the more important market for developing country borrowers .

The US Capital Markets

The US still has the most stringent regulatory climate. One hurdle for developing country sovereign and public entity borrowers is the Security Act of 1933, which requires all issuers of bonds to register with the Securities and Exchange Commission (SEC). Thus developing countries have mostly tapped the institutional markets and raised money via private placements or bonds under the new Rule 144a, neither of which requires SEC registration. Disclosure requirements are thus similar to those in the Eurobond markets. Without reporting requirements, it is impossible to qualify the total volume of new issues in these two markets. But it can be assumed that a total of US$100 - 150 billion was raised annually at the end of the 1980s. It is with this number in mind that the relative unimportance of developing country issues can be seen. Their volume was probably only around 1% of the total for 1989. (And private placements are generally only about 35% of the overall new issue activity.)[39] To enhance the standing of the private placement market and to increase transparency, the Rule 144a market was created.

Rule 144a opened the new issues market in the US for borrowers who want to avoid the process of an SEC filing. Investors in this market must manage assets in excess of US$ 100 million to participate, a requirement that excludes retail investors. As listing and disclosure requirements are less stringent, the market is limited to those investors who can independently evaluate the issuer's credit risk. The main difference with the private placement market is the tradability of the bonds, which helps to tighten yields, giving borrowers better conditions in the form of lower yields.

There are various reasons for institutions to buy Third World debt. The first is risk-reward: the high yield of the transactions is perceived to surpass the risk. Because investors would normally invest only a very small portion of their portfolio in developing country assets, the risk remains manageable—while at the same time increasing the total yield of the portfolios. Second, some asset managers who had invested in high-yield corporate bonds, the troubled junk bonds, are now looking for alternative high-yielding instruments. Third, investors could, at least initially, realize considerable capital gains as the issues traded down in yields. As the examples of Mexican issuers showed, the first issues had to be more generously priced to arouse investor demand; subsequent demand by a growing group of investors brought the yields down. Fourth, once a fund takes the decision to do a credit evaluation of an issuer and its country of origin, it is likely that, provided the outcome is positive, the fund will participate in several issues once it is familiar with the name. Institutional investors thus bought paper from more than one Mexican public entity. Fifth, developing country names were in some cases introduced through securitized structures. It is not a big step to buy straight Mexican debt, after having purchased a securitized deal. Finally, Mexico at least is geographically close to the US, which makes it easier for fund managers to "track". It will probably be some time before US institutions are ready to purchase Eastern European debt.

---

39   Melvin Rines, US Dollar, Euromoney Guide to International Capital Markets, London, 1989, p. 177ff

The Yankee market is the SEC-regulated market for foreign bond issues. Its volume, typically less than US $10 billion each year, has been rather limited in comparison with the overall US capital markets. Developing country borrowers have generally avoided the market, mainly because of its difficult and costly registration requirements. The advantage of SEC registration is that private investors are also allowed to buy the issues, which reduces the yields on average by 5 to 10 basis points relative to the private placement market. In addition, the participation of individual investors guarantees broader distribution and firmer placement. As private investors participate in the market, the name recognition is more important in that it makes it easier for Asian or Latin American sovereigns than for East European states to tap the Yankee market.

The most prominent recent example is Thailand, which launched a US$200 million 10-year issue in the Yankee market, lead-managed by Salomon Brothers and J.P. Morgan and underwritten by a strong syndicate group. The issue proved to be a success, so that Thailand can be expected to tap the market again. Private investors participated in the issue, which was reported to be broadly distributed. One factor influencing the success is the fact that Thailand carries a rating by Standard and Poors of A-[40] and is thus classified as investment grade.[41] This is important as investors in the US markets tend to look at ratings far more than do investors in the Eurobond markets.

The Eurobond Markets

The Eurobond markets are very mature with a vast investor base and great liquidity. New issue activity was US$160 billion in 1990.[42] The market is not confined by European borders; Middle and Far Eastern as well as Latin American investors have traditionally participated. In general, Eurobonds need not be registered and are traded in the major financial centers. As bonds are mostly in bearer form, it is most difficult to determine the ownership profile of a particular issue. Listing, which is normally done in Luxembourg (Frankfurt for DM issues, Zürich for Swiss Franc (SFR) bonds), is a formality. But, the issuer has to publish a prospectus with financial details. The US dollar has traditionally been the most active currency, followed by the SFR and DM. For developing countries, the DM and the US dollar were the most important issuing currencies. For that reason, our analysis will focus on investors in these markets.

The DM Eurobond Market. The DM has long been an important issuing currency for developing country borrowers. The success of the DM market for developing country borrowers is based is on this fact: no issuer has ever defaulted in the German bond market. Even in the most difficult times, developing country borrowers have punctually serviced their debt. Although the market is based in Germany, the investor profile is greatly varied. Domestic retail investors are the major participants, independent of the issuer, but German institutions, European retail investors, (the Belgian Dentist), Middle and Far Eastern investors, and Latin American investors all participate. We thus differentiate among the investor groups.

German retail investors have bought Mexican issues, bonds issued by the Republic of Turkey, and India, Algeria, and Eastern European names. Since German investors have not had any bad experience with developing country debt, the bonds are perceived to be relatively safe investments. While the high coupon, which nowadays reaches double-digit figures, compensates for the extra risk, the most important point is that defaults or even payment delays are unknown in

---

40   As a matter of interest, Greece, a member of the European Community, is rated BBB (implicit rating) thus ranking below Thailand.

41   A-1 long term, and A1 short term.

42   IFR, No. 859, January 5, 1991

contrast, for example, to the US corporate debt market. Thus it is not surprising that investors did not dump their Mexican paper at the beginning of the 1980s, when Mexico experienced difficulties. These same investors are among the buyers of the newest group.

Eastern European names are a special case. Under their communist regimes, these countries had an impeccable record for debt repayment.[43] Their proximity to Germany, with its traditional links to Eastern Europe, enabled countries like Hungary, Bulgaria, and the Soviet Union to tap these markets using not only syndicated loans but bond issues as well. In addition, since the mid-70s, investors had believed in the so-called umbrella theory which supposedly held that if a Comecon country found itself unable to service its debt, the Soviet Union would bail it out. Since the revolutions of 1989, the various debtors have been judged by their individual credit standing. This means that the markets are closed for most borrowers except Hungary and Czechoslovakia.

A special market segment has developed for bonds issued by Turkey, which have been purchased to a certain extent by Turkish resident workers who have their income denominated in DM and prefer to keep their savings in Germany.

German institutions have been more risk-averse than the retail investors, although they also participated in developing country issues to increase the return on their investment portfolios. Thus, in addition to the issues by Asian borrowers, a certain percentage of the recent DM Eurobonds for Mexico, Hungary, and Czechoslovakia have been placed with German institutional investors.

With the DM traditionally a strong currency, DM bonds have been purchased by other European retail investors with accounts both in Germany and abroad. Furthermore, a certain percentage of issues has been placed in Switzerland, where it is difficult to determine the nationality of the end-investor.

Next to European retail investors, European institutional investors have been the most active participants in these markets. They have bought Asian Eurobonds frequently, as well as some of the recent Mexico Eurobonds.

Banks have purchased developing country paper and swapped the fixed-rate obligations into floating-rate obligations. This is particularly true for foreign banks with a seat in Germany that do only limited direct lending to corporates; they can increase their assets by purchasing bonds in combination with a swap in so-called asset swap packages, thus matching their asset and liability structure. Developing country borrowers are ideal for asset swaps. Not many other bonds trade at 1% (and more) yield margins over the DM swap rates. The developing country bonds can thus translate into a margin of more than 1% over DM Libor. By using this method the banks could not circumvent general credit limits for developing countries, but in some instances, the fact that the bonds were in the form of a bearer Eurobond in some instances put them into a different credit category.

Latin American retail investors with accounts in both Europe and their home countries are said to have played a major role in the recent wave of new issues for Latin American borrowers. The exact amounts purchased are difficult to estimate, since these investors could have obtained the bonds through accounts in Germany, Switzerland, or Luxembourg, or directly in their home countries. As the bonds are in bearer form, they cannot be easily traced.

In the 1980s, the appetite for bonds grew in the Middle East, where both institutions and private investors have been buying Eurobonds. Bonds for developing country

---

43   Even Romania paid back all its debt (under conditions of tremendous hardship for the people and the economy).

borrowers have been purchased mainly by institutional investors. DM issues (and even ASCH issues) have been bought, sometimes in substantial blocks, although most of the demand has been for US dollar-denominated paper. Of the recent Mexican issues, a certain percentage is supposed to have been placed in the Middle East, although demand dried up with the onset of the Gulf crisis.

It is difficult to calculate the general percentage distribution of the DM issues of developing country borrowers, as they are in bearer form. To say that a certain number of bonds was sold in Switzerland, for example, does not necessarily mean that Swiss nationals were the investors. Not only can the bonds be placed in accounts of foreign nationals, they can also be held in managed funds or sold on to other countries, like the Middle or Far East, without any direct records.

A typical DM Eurobond for a Latin American borrower can be assumed to have the following approximate distribution:

German retail investors	40%
German institutional investors	15%
European retail investors[44]:	20%
European institutional investors	10%
Latin American retail investors[45]:	10%
Japanese institutional investors	2%
Middle East institutional investors	3%

In general, the distribution depends on the country of origin of the issuer, the placing power of the lead manager of the bond issue, and the strength of the underwriting group. DM bonds for Asian borrowers are likely to be sold within Germany, with other European private and institutional investors participating. Latin American bonds to some extent are likely to flow back into Latin American accounts, although it is doubtful whether more than one-quarter of a DM issue will be bought by Latin American investors. The majority of developing country bonds is likely to end up in retail accounts.

The US Dollar Eurobond Market. The US dollar-based Eurobond market for developing countries is more diversified with regard to the investor base. US dollar Eurobonds are in bearer form, too, so the exact distribution and placement are not known. Institutional investors are far more prominent. Due to the weakness of the dollar, European retail investors have recently been reluctant to buy US dollar-denominated bonds, a phenomenon unrelated to the developing country issuers. An interesting distinction in this market is between fixed-rate bonds and floating-rate notes. Whereas the fixed-rate bond market remained relatively closed during the 1980s, many developing country issuers were able to tap the floating-rate market, normally dominated by institutional investors. Since 1988, however, there has been a wave of new fixed-rate issues for both Latin American and Asian borrowers.

US institutions can participate in the Eurobond markets through their off-shore affiliates. As these institutions follow very stringent investment criteria, only a small portion of their assets would be invested in developing country bonds. Like US domestic institutions, these investors' focus is on Latin American and Asian borrowers; Eastern Europe seems to be excluded at present. Japanese institutions have stayed largely on the sidelines and have not been major buyers of developing country debt in the Euromarkets. It can be assumed that the total participation in recent developing country bond issues was less than 5%.

---

44 Includes Latin American accounts in Europe.
45 Accounts held in Latin America.

A typical US dollar Eurobond for Latin American borrowers would be distributed in the following way:

European retail investors[46]	25%
Latin American retail investors[47]	20%
European institutional investors	30%
US institutional investors[48]	15%
Japanese institutional investors	5%
Middle East institutional investors[49]	5%

Once the East European countries do more to overcome their economic difficulties, the investor base for these names will widen and will increasingly include US and Far Eastern institutional investors.

The Samurai and Yen Private Placement Markets

Throughout the past decade, developing country borrowers have been issuing in the Samurai markets to obtain medium to long-term fixed-rate funding.[50] Latin American names were almost totally absent between 1986 and spring 1990, although countries with similar or worse credit standings managed to obtain funds.[51] Issuing activity remained concentrated on East European, Asian, and Caribbean names, with borrowers as diverse as the Bank of China, Czechoslovakia Obchodni Banka, Barbados, and Trinidad and Tobago. Investors in these markets are almost exclusively institutions—ife insurance companies, regional and city banks, trust banks, and other insurance and small financial institutions. Some government agencies have also participated as investors.

Samurai issues need to carry Ministry of Finance approval and be registered. They should also be rated, by either US or local Japanese ratings agencies (which have quite different criteria), with a minimum single "A." The market is very illiquid and secondary trading is nonexistent for most issues since investors treat their assets as long-term holdings.

Some smaller issues, listed here under the classification of Samurai, are in fact held by one or two institutions and are therefore de facto private placements. Most of these are handled privately, but some issues are reported.[52]

The basic problem facing this market segment now is the lack of funds and the unwillingness of Japanese institutional investors to consider borrowers of lesser risk. Institutions have been busy investing in developing country names through yen private placements or Samurai issues (and direct loans) for a good part of the 1980s, so that the most of them have now reached

---

46   This group would very likely include Latin American accounts in Europe.

47   Bonds bought directly via the retail branch networks of the respective underwriters or from local brokers.

48   Off-shore.

49   Mostly institutions.

50   The Samurai market is the Japanese yen public bond market in Tokyo for foreign issuers. Most developing country borrowers tapped these markets on a private placement basis. cf. also below.

51   There was one issue for the Republic of Colombia: five years, Y 6 billion, 6.9% coupon, priceed at par, lead-manager by Nomura.

52   As one of the latest issues, Nikko arranged a Yen 3.75 billion 5-year deal with a 6.7% coupon for the Republic of Uruguay, a borrower who has not managed to tap any other bond market so far.

the limits of their credit lines to developing country countries. This problem is most pronounced in Eastern Europe, where Japanese institutions and banks acted as lenders on a large scale before the various revolutions. Now that the new governments desperately need new funds to restructure their economies, credit lines are full, and no new money can be mobilized. The problem is, of course, exacerbated by the impact of the collapse of the Japanese equity and real estate markets on banks' and institutions' balance sheets.

8. A SUGGESTED APPROACH FOR TAPPING THE INTERNATIONAL BOND MARKETS

Commercial banks lent vast amounts of money to developing countries for general financing, mostly unrelated to specific projects, in the years after the first oil crisis and into the 1980s. Bonds, by contrast, have always been a minor part of developing country debt, one of the main reasons they have not been included in the restructurings of that debt. And the fact that bond issues have always been punctually serviced is the main reason the markets have remained open for some borrowers and reopened for others, notably Mexico. This background must be kept in mind when we evaluate prospects for developing countries raising funds in the international capital markets. In this section, we discuss factors important for successfully tapping the markets. We begin with issues to be faced by those borrowers that are not yet at the first stage of the process and continue with issues for borrowers whose bonds are already held by investors.

Preliminaries

The key factor distinguishing developing countries with and without access to international bond markets will continue to be investors' perceptions of economic management. For a country starting out on the path to establishing creditworthiness, a necessary (but probably not sufficient) proxy for sound economic management, from the market's viewpoint, is adherence to some type of adjustment program. Before making a successful debut in the international bond markets, a country must demonstrate prudent economic management, gain control over its fiscal deficit, achieve a "neutral" policy environment which allows both domestic and foreign investors to perceive risks and rewards at their appropriate market valuations, and demonstrate a general level of economic "health" so it is not seen as dependent on transfusions of foreign savings. In other words, the less the apparent need, the more readily will it be able to attract voluntary funds.[53] This is borne out by experience.

Most successful borrowers in the international capital markets, including those which temporarily lost access and have successfully reentered, have implemented most, if not all, of the following economic measures: [54]

- Liberalized and substantially deregulated their economies
- Increased the role of the private sector
- Encouraged foreign direct investment
- Shifted from import substitution to exports as the engine of growth
- Improved current account performance
- Improved political stability indicators
- Reduced fiscal deficits.

A lesson worth restating from the recent past is that countries should refrain from increasing borrowings in response to a windfall from commodity price increases, unless the proceeds are sure to be invested in foreign-exchange-generating activities. Such a windfall is likely to attract an unstable supply of speculative funds from retail investors who are looking for short-term, high-risk profit opportunities from the commodity boom. It is not a sound basis for attracting long-term foreign bond savings. When it comes to accepting bonds from a new issuer, there is clearly a learning curve in the investment community. Most developing countries do not have natural links at the retail level with a developed country capital market (such a link is the most

---

53 Enclave projects or those fully secured abroad may be partial exceptions.
54 China, India, and former COMECON countries are notable exceptions.

plausible explanation for Czechoslovakia's recent successful tapping of the German bond market, for example), and must recognize that there are unavoidable "set-up costs" when tapping investors for the first time. Early issues will probably have to be of short maturity, modest in size (manageable even in a worst-case scenario), and priced rather generously to attract investors' attention and overcome the "unknown borrower" factor or, worse, the "recently uncreditworthy borrower" factor. For borrowers from developing countries with little or no track record, investors will also demand securitized issues or substantial collateral. A developing country that wants bond market financing must consider such costs to be quasi-marketing expenses necessary to introduce its name to investors' portfolios.

Need for a Strategy and a Well-Defined Institutional Entity

For newcomers to the capital markets, the most fundamental confidence-builder that will separate one-time entrants from those who will be able to establish a successful track record is the developing country's debt management and external borrowing strategy. A measure of progress is the ability to obtain improved borrowing terms for successive issues. Developing countries would benefit from a well-defined institutional structure that would maintain close links with the foreign financial community and orchestrate and negotiate all public foreign borrowings. The primary task of the entity would be to take the lead in lowering the benchmark borrowing terms for all borrowers from that particular developing country. This is done through a series of actions outlined below. The relative importance of each action will clearly change as countries become more experienced in tapping the markets, but any action must remain the responsibility of the public sector entity.

Annual Borrowing Ceilings. Most frequent borrowers in the international capital markets announce, at the beginning of their financial year, their ceiling on annual capital market borrowing and, more important, they keep to it. Ideally, this would set the ceiling for the developing countries' entire public debt, averting a situation when the state borrows indirectly via state-owned enterprises or regional entities. Initially, this ceiling would have to be rather low for new developing country entrants, to avoid "flooding" the market with new issues from one particular country and thus damaging longer-term relations. Furthermore, by limiting the amount of paper outstanding, the perceived exclusivity of bond borrowings is maintained. Such a strategy also gives investors an impression of financial discipline. The immediate result can be expected to be better borrowing terms, since more investors will have confidence in the country—leading to more demand and, consequently, lower yields.

Markets to Tap. The question of which market to tap is important, as it determines not only the investor base but also the structure of the bonds and the information required to launch the issue.

The Euromarkets guarantee very wide distribution, with relatively limited disclosure requirements; bonds are in bearer form. The wider the investor base, the more demand for the issues, and potentially, the lower the yield. If an issue for a similar borrower, albeit from a different country, is already trading in the market, it could serve as a benchmark.

The public bond market in the US offers the greatest liquidity and flexibility for US dollar-denominated funding. In the US, public bonds must be registered with the SEC, which has very strict and complicated registering and disclosure requirements. Still, borrowers, especially sovereigns, should consider pursuing this market because of its depth. This is particularly true if a country seeks a permanent reentry into the international capital markets. The ability to tap the US domestic public market would add another dimension to a developing country's borrowing prospects. As the registration requirements are easier to fulfill for sovereigns, the Yankee market would be more appropriate for developing countries issuing bonds in their own name.

An alternative, especially for public entities and private borrowers, for whom the registration procedures would be too cumbersome, could be the newly created Rule 144a market, in which US institutions are allowed to purchase bonds without SEC registration. This market, which only extends the flexibility and tradability of private placements, is based on the multibillion dollar demand of institutional investors and could thus be an addition to the Euromarket.

It should be noted, however, that retail investors are likeliest to hold a bond to maturity, even if unfavorable economic developments occur following the bond issue. One explanation is that transactions costs are too high for a retail investor to restructure his portfolio frequently; another is that the investor is not as likely to be aware of the latest developments unless they make headlines. Institutional and high net worth investors are more likely to shift out of a particular country's paper before maturity in response to economic developments. Large volumes make transactions costs less of an obstacle to frequent portfolio restructuring, and allow immediate profit-taking when there are opportunities to realize capital gains.

The Samurai or yen private placement markets do not offer the same liquidity and size as the Euromarket or the US markets. However, especially if the borrower requires yen funding, this market would be ideal. A yen private placement can be considered for small issues, which would be bought by one or two Japanese institutions.

Public Relations. Obviously, a developing country borrower that wants wide distribution of its bonds must conduct a major marketing drive. The developing country must provide accurate and timely information regarding economic developments, so that private investors and credit analysts in institutions can track the country. Major "roadshows" covering the important investor centers would be a precondition of successful issues and should be aimed at both institutional and retail investors. Successful borrowers tend to hold roadshows annually.[55]

Institutional investors and private bankers will be interested in the economic fundamentals, general creditworthiness, and overall borrowing strategy and ceilings. They will also want to know the developing country's institutional arrangement for managing existing debt and new borrowings. Institutional investors' identities are easily accessible, and the countries can disseminate the most relevant information and try to influence handily how it is perceived. A direct contact to certain institutional investors will also provide feedback about the market in general and the specific borrower's standing in particular.

Issue Structures. The institutional entity responsible for managing the country's entry into the bond markets should also keep track of all public sector issue structures and serve as a source of information. While it should not become involved in the structuring of private sector deals, it should keep track of them whenever possible. Publication of issue structures in an official gazette or a special newsletter will make the information on improved borrowing terms widely accessible to private borrowers who may then benefit from this source of funding. The entity should also pursue financial information on public sector borrowers who are planning to issue bonds, and develop some estimate of their creditworthiness based on domestic disclosure guidelines.

If a country intends to tap the markets frequently, its issues should not be too tightly priced. Such issues tend to trade up in yields so that the country's borrowing costs are likely to be higher in the long run.

---

55 Roadshows are organized by the leadmanager and are done by many prime borrowers (including the World Bank) who would be represented by their private bankers.

Initially issuers will have to structure their borrowings to give investors confidence. This implies that first issues are likely to have short maturities, semiannual or even quarterly coupons, amortization schedules (versus bullet maturities), or put options for the investors. These technical structures bring down the duration of the issues.[56]

Private sector borrowers are likely to have to provide collateral or guarantees for their first borrowings to fulfill investors' credit requirements. In some existing issues, the pledging of off-shore holdings provides the necessary guarantee, especially when there is the probability that payment restrictions in the home country of the borrower might prevent the payment of interest and principal.

Credit Rating. Ratings from US agencies are useful once a country has substantially completed its economic adjustment process. Standard & Poors and Moody's are the two US rating agencies that give borrowers either direct or implicit ratings.[57] As a high percentage of investors look at formal credit ratings, obtaining such a rating would help a borrower—unless it fell well below investment grade.

Standard & Poors, for example, rates sovereign governments, including developing countries. A formal rating is undertaken only at the request of the borrower,[58] and need not be accepted if the borrower does not agree with S&P's opinion. In that event, the rating would remain unpublished. Ratings are given for long-term and short-term debt but, in this context, only the long-term debt is of interest.[59] S&P has two basic categories, "investment grade" and "speculative grade." Investment grade ratings are AAA, AA, A, and BBB; speculative grade would be BB, B, CCC, CC, C and D (default).[60] In 1989 the following developing countries were either explicitly (e) or implicitly (i) rated by S & P as follows:

Singapore	AA	(i)
Taiwan	AA	(i)
Hong Kong	A+	(i)
Malaysia	A-	(i)
South Korea	A+	(i)
Thailand	A-	(e)
Israel	BBB-	(i)
India	BBB	(i)
Venezuela	B+	(e)

---

56 Which has the practical implication, that the investor receives his money back earlier.

57 Implicit ratings do not refer to a particular stock of debt and are done without the request of the country.

58 The borrower has to pay the cost of the rating.

59 Short term debt would cover CP programs etc.

60 "Debt rated "BB" "B" "CCC" "CC" and "C" is regarded as having predominantly speculative characteristics with respect to capacity to pay interest and repay principal. "BB" indicates the least degree of speculation, "C" the highest. While such debt will likely have some quality and protective characteristics, these are outweighed by large uncertainties or major exposures to adverse conditions. S&P Credit Review, June 26, 1990.

Moody's[61] has given the following sovereign foreign currency debt ratings to developing countries :[62]

Singapore[63]	Aa3
Korea	A1
India[64]	A2
Thailand	A2
Hong Kong[65]	A3
Malaysia	A3
China	Baa1
Hungary	Ba1
Mexico	Ba2
Venezuela	Ba3
Brazil[66]:	B2
Argentina	B3

No entity within a country can obtain a higher rating than the implicit or explicit rating of the sovereign government.[67]

Sequencing. Below, we suggest a series of steps to be taken, in turn, by first time public sector borrowers who wish to obtain access to the international bond markets as a strategic, long-term objective and get better terms for bond finance:

1. A perfect record on repayment of short-term letters of credit, suppliers' credit, and other expensive trade-related facilities.

2. Issuance of a small volume of two- to three-year notes with an amortization schedule to reduce the notes' duration. Quarterly or semiannual interest payments and/or put options for investors, government guaranteed. Or,

3. Alternatively, a four-to five-year securitized issue with an amortization schedule.

4. A five year government guaranteed issue with bullet maturity.

5. Unguaranteed medium-term bond issues by public sector enterprises.

Private borrowers would follow a similar sequence of steps, except that they would also be able to provide offshore collateral to back their bond issues.

---

61 Moody's follows a slightly different numbering, ranging from Aaa, via Aa1-3, A1-3, Baa1-3, Ba1-3 to B1-3. To give a comparison, Baa1 to Baa3 would roughly correspond to S&P A - BBB - ratings. The two rating agencies have their separate criteria so that the same borrower can obtain (slightly) different ratings.

62 Moody's Investor Service: Sovereign Foreign Currency Debt Ratings, September 12, 1990.

63 Sovereign ceiling rating -- no central government or government guaranteed debt rated.

64 Rating under review for possible downgrade.

65 Sovereign ceiling rating -- no central government or government guaranteed debt rated.

66 New money bonds.

67 Except by using off shore or securitized structures as collateral.

9. ISSUES FOR FUTURE BORROWING

Distinction between Bank Debt and Brady Bonds

The primary aims of developing country issuers already in the market are to keep access open, to lengthen maturities, and to reduce spreads. They can achieve these through a solid track record and substantial investor demand. During the debt crisis of the 1980s, the clear cut distinction between bank debt, which can be rescheduled, and bonds, which are kept out of the rescheduling process, kept the international capital markets open as a source for new funds. Thanks to the differentiation between the two kinds of debt instruments, a developing country in financial difficulty could still keep a window open for additional small-scale borrowings.

The crucial issue, however, is whether countries can continue to assure the seniority of new issue sovereign bond obligations once they have large volumes of former bank debt now outstanding in the form of Brady bonds. If countries assure seniority of all outstanding bonds, what will this imply for (1) other creditors, (2) the yields of Brady bonds and (3) the terms of future new sovereign issues?

For issuers with large volumes of Brady bonds outstanding, it is essential to differentiate direct new issues in the minds of investors. While the rationale for Brady bonds was precisely to convert bank loans into tradable instruments, it is nevertheless to the debtor's advantage if such trading were to take place exclusively within the commercial banking community, thus leaving institutional and retail investors open to holding new paper from direct issues.

Enhancements

Another area of concern for borrowers accessing the market with the help of enhancements such as offshore collateral, securitized issues, or World Bank guarantees is the extent to which they can eventually graduate from such assistance and obtain favorable terms on their own merits. Experience has proved that the use of offshore collateral or securitization (in the sense of deals that are backed with the borrower's own foreign currency-denominated assets, such as receivables) is probably both necessary and desirable in reestablishing creditworthiness. But once the country has established a track record of prompt payments, it can reduce and eventually eliminate the need for such aid.

Market Saturation

Despite the positive development of renewed issuing activity at the end of 1989 and the beginning of 1990, it should not be overlooked that the market for developing country bonds is limited, with a very small investor base that is increasing slowly. This market is therefore easily saturated. In Germany, demand has recently been slowing down for Latin American names. As a result, investors may focus increasingly on prime developing country borrowers, making it difficult for second-tier borrowers to tap the markets unless they are willing to pay a high yield. In the case of saturation, there are only two options for the borrower (1) to wait until more demand develops, which could mean waiting until the implicit credit standing improves—a slow process, or (2) to diversify into other markets.

Exogenous Factors

A developing country's success in raising voluntary finance through bond markets depends heavily on its perceived vulnerability to exogenous factors which influence its ability to service its debt. Reliable access to foreign exchange through current account surpluses is at risk for countries whose imports or exports are concentrated in a narrow range of products or geographic markets. For example, several newly industrializing economies in Asia are vulnerable to sharp contractions in their key export markets if the US and other industrial countries undergo a recession or adopt protectionist legislation. The same holds true for the impact of imports on the balance of payments. Countries whose imports are concentrated in critical goods, which are unavailable domestically and cannot be substituted (energy or food), also face external payment risks.[68] Technological changes in industrial nations can unexpectedly depress worldwide demand for nonfood agricultural commodities which often represent the bulk of a developing country's exports.

For example, petroleum-based synthetic products have exercised strong downward pressure on natural rubber and natural fibre (cotton, jute, wool) prices since the mid-1950s. The oil shocks of the 1970s, 1980s, and even 1990 do not seem to have significantly modified the downward direction of the prices of nonfood agricultural commodities relative to those of manufactures.[69]

In most cases, the most important service import category in the balance of payments is the interest payment on external debt. The impact of adverse interest and exchange rate movements is magnified for short-maturity, floating-rate obligations. Foreign exchange earnings from services, including tourism, are likewise vulnerable to exchange rate movements.

The capital account can be adversely affected by reduced foreign investor confidence, forcing a country to draw down limited foreign exchange reserves. Political instability and deterioration of economic conditions can also lead to portfolio disinvestment and large-scale capital flight by domestic investors. In most circumstances governments may prefer to finance their deficits domestically, since repayments on external borrowing come with the added uncertainties of exchange rate movements, shifts in the terms of trade and other developments over which they have little control.

It follows from this that current account deficits—associated with imprudently managed imports and foreign borrowings, resulting in relatively high consumption and falling rates of net investment—would be likely to have an adverse impact on the country's creditworthiness and hence its future access to the capital markets. Many developing countries that found their access to overseas borrowing restricted in the mid to late 1980s had earlier experienced foreign-financed consumption, which increased external debt but did not improve their capacity to service foreign obligations.

State of the Capital Markets

Even if a country has an effective macroeconomic adjustment program in place and the macroeconomic variables are showing improvement, there are times when it cannot count on the international capital markets as sources of new funds. Developments after the invasion of Kuwait demonstrate this. In the spring of 1990 the investment climate was excellent, and the many new issues launched for developing country borrowers proved there was substantial investor demand in the various markets. After the invasion of Kuwait, however, this demand dried up, as investors moved into higher cash positions and better-quality names. Similarly, the fall of the Japanese equity market and declining real estate prices have led to a sharp cutback in investment activities by Japanese institutions, to the detriment of developing countries that had planned to tap these markets. In general, it is believed that these two developments have not completely shut the window for developing country borrowers and that demand will return soon.

---

68 The impact of higher oil prices on almost all developing countries as a result of the annexation of Kuwait illustrates this point.

69 E.R. Grilli & M.C. Yang, WBER, Jan. 88, Vol.2 No.1.

Conclusion

The international capital markets have emerged as a small but not insignificant source of new funds for developing country borrowers. The market share for developing country issues remains limited, mainly because there is direct competition for funds with corporate and public sector borrowers from developed countries, and with multilateral institutions. Developing country bonds will be considered only for a very small, high-risk portion of the investment portfolio. Other candidates for this risky niche are second and third tier corporate borrowers of developed countries. The recent difficulties of sovereigns in servicing commercial bank loans naturally raise questions in the minds of potential investors regarding their ability to maintain uninterrupted service on bond debt. As discussed above, time will tell whether the impact of large volumes of Brady bonds outstanding helps or harms the prospect of additional new issues of sovereign obligations. The volatile access to the international capital markets should also be kept in mind. Exogenous developments very often rearrange investors' perceptions of acceptable risk-reward, which results in developing country issuers being abruptly locked out of the market. Even the few developing countries that have managed to overcome all of the obstacles discussed in this paper, and have issued bonds on successively improving terms, would be well advised to limit their borrowings voluntarily to easily manageable levels given the seniority and inflexibility of this instrument.

If developing countries take a cautious approach in gradually building a track record, and if and when they show success in their macroeconomic adjustment process, more of them will be in a position to tap these markets. In addition, with a broadening of the investor base, countries already in the markets will find these sources of fresh funds for their economic development ever more significant and stable. It is expected that, while the absolute level of sustainable borrowing will continue to be determined endogenously for any developing country, the composition of such borrowed funds will shift gradually to include a greater role for private sector voluntary funds, as developing country economies become more integrated with those of the developed countries.

DEBT TYPE	ISSUE SIZE/ PRICE	BORROWER	ISSUE DATE	COUPON/ LAUNCH YIELD	UNDERWRITER	SECURITY/ GUARANTEE	MARKET	COMMENTS
ALGERIA								
US$ FLOATING:	US$100m/ NA	Sonatrach	3/90 - 3/97	LIBOR + 1.00%/ NA	Chase	NA	EURO	
DM:	DM200m/ NA	Banque Exterieure d'Algerie	7/86 - 7/92	6.75%/ NA	DG Bank/BAII	NA	EURO	
	DM150m/ 100	Banque Nationale d'Algerie	3/88 - 3/94	6.25%/ NA	Dresdner Bank	NA	EURO	
	DM150M/ 100	Banque Exterieure d'Algerie	9/88 - 9/93	7.00%/ NA	DG Bank	NA	EURO	
	DM150m/ NA	Banque Exterieure d'Algerie	5/89 - 5/94	7.75%/ NA	DG Bank/BAII	NA	EURO	
	DM150m/ 100	Banque Exterieure d'Algerie	8/89 - 4/94	7.75%/ NA	BHF Bank	NA	EURO	
	DM150m/ NA	Banque Nationale d'Algerie	8/89 - 8/94	8.50%/ NA	BHF Bank	NA	EURO	
	DM50m/ 100	Sonelglaz	2/90 - 2/95	9.50%/ NA	BHF Bank	NA	EURO	
YEN:	¥10bn/ 100	Banque Exterieure d'Algerie	3/86 - 10/95	6.60%/ NA	IBJ	NA	SAMURAI/PP	
	¥10bn/ 100	Banque Exterieure d'Algerie	4/86 - 11/94	6.80%/ NA	IBJ	NA	SAMURAI/PP	
	¥8bn/ 100	Banque Nationale d'Algerie	5/86 - 5/93	6.50%/ NA	Nomura	NA	SAMURAI/PP	
	¥8bn/ 100	Banque Nationale d'Algerie	5/86 - 4/95	6.40%/ NA	Nikko	NA	SAMURAI/PP	
	¥7bn/ 100	Credit Populaire d'Algerie	10/86 - 10/94	6.60%/ NA	Tokai	NA	SAMURAI/PP	
	¥8bn	Credit Populaire d'Algerie	10/86 - 5/95	6.40%/ NA	Nikko	NA	SAMURAI/PP	
	¥8bn/ 100	Banque Nationale d'Algerie	3/88 - 3/95	6.4%/ NA	Nikko	NA	SAMURAI/PP	
SFR:	SFr60m/ NA	Banque Algerienne de Development	11/86 - 11/96	LIBOR + 0.50%/ NA	Swiss Bank Corporation	NA	EURO	
ARGENTINA								
US$ FIXED:	$26m/ NA	Molinos Rio de la Plata	12/90 - 12/95	11.00%/ 14.50%	Merrill Lynch & Banco Frances	Unsecured	EURO	·$21m of this bond is sold worldwide at the fixed 11.00%, but $5m will be issued domestically at LIBOR +4.6%
US$ FLOATING:	$195m/ 50	Banco Nacionale Argentina	11/87 - 10/97	LIBOR + 0.75%/ NA	IBJ International	Government Guarantee	EURO	
BARBADOS								
YEN:	¥4.3bn/ 100	Barbados	5/86 - 10/91	6.90%/ NA	Nikko	NA	SAMURAI/PP	
	¥5bn/ 100	Barbados	5/86 - 5/98	6.80%/ NA	Nomura	NA	SAMURAI/PP	
STERLING:	£30m/ 99	Barbados	12/90 - 7/15	13.50%/ 13.65%	BZW	NA	EURO	

DEBT TYPE	ISSUE SIZE/ PRICE	BORROWER	ISSUE DATE	COUPON/ LAUNCH YIELD	UNDERWRITER	SECURITY/ GUARANTEE	MARKET	COMMENTS
BRAZIL								
US$ FIXED:	US$250m/ 94.0388	Petroleo Brasileiro (PETROBAS)	8/91 - 8/93	10.00%/ 13.50%	Chase Manhattan	Unsecured	EURO	• First issue by Brazil since early 1980's • Call option after one year @ 97.0699
BULGARIA								
DM:	DM200m/ 100	Bulgarian Foreign Trade Bank	6/89 - 6/96	8.50%/ NA	Bayerische Vereinsbank	NA	EURO	
YEN:	¥6bn/ 100	Bulgarian Foreign Trade Bank	5/86 - 11/99	5.90%/ NA	IBJ	NA	SAMURAI/PP	
	¥10bn/ 100	Bulgarian Foreign Trade Bank	5/86 - 12/98	5.70%/ NA	Bank of Tokyo	NA	SAMURAI/PP	
	¥10bn/ 100	Bulgarian Foreign Trade Bank	5/86 - 3/99	5.80%/ NA	Nikko	NA	SAMURAI/PP	
	¥5bn/ 100	Mineral Bank of Bulgaria	2/89 - 6/96	5.80%/ NA	IBJ	NA	SAMURAI/PP	
CHILE								
US$ FLOATING:	US$320m/ NA	Chile	3/91 - 3/96 (two years grace)	LIBOR + 1.50%/ NA	Manufacturers Hanover	NA	EURO (quasi voluntary)	• This bond was issued to banks as a refinancing of commercial bank debt
CHINA								
US$ FIXED:	US$50m/ 100.5	Guangdong Int'l Trust Investment	6/87 - 6/92	8.50%/ NA	Chemical Asia	NA	EURO	
	US$100m/ 101.5	Bank of Communications	7/88 - 7/93	9.375%/ NA	Daiwa Singapore	NA	EURO	
US$ FLOATING:	US$200m/ 100	Bank of China	7/86 - 7/96	Variable/ NA	Deutsche Bank	NA	EURO	
	US$200m/ 100	Bank of China	5/87 - 5/97	Variable/ NA	Daiwa Singapore	NA	EURO	
	US$200m/ 100	Bank of China	10/87 - 10/92	Variable/ NA	Warburg Securities	NA	EURO	
DM:	DM300m/ 100	People's Republic of China	10/87 - 10/92	6.00%/ NA	Dresdner Bank	NA	EURO	
	DM200m/ 100	Bank of China	10/88 - 10/93	3M LIBOR+0.0625%/ NA	Commerzbank	NA	EURO	•Floating
YEN:	¥25bn/ 100	Shanghai Ivestment & Trust Corp.	1/86 - 5/96	6.60%/ NA	Daiwa Securities	NA	SAMURAI/PP	
	¥15bn/ 99.7	Bank of China	2/86 - 2/92	5.20%/ NA	Nikko	NA	SAMURAI/PP	
	¥20bn/ 101.35	Bank of China	2/86 - 4/99	5.30%/ NA	Nomura	NA	SAMURAI/PP	
	¥40bn/ 99.7	China Int'l Trust & Investment Corp	2/86 - 2/96	6.30%/ NA	Daiwa Securities	NA	SAMURAI/PP	
	¥20bn/ 101.5	Bank of China	3/86 - 4/96	7.20%/ NA	Nikko	NA	SAMURAI/PP	

DEBT TYPE	ISSUE SIZE/ PRICE	BORROWER	ISSUE DATE	COUPON/ LAUNCH YIELD	UNDERWRITER	SECURITY/ GUARANTEE	MARKET	COMMENTS
	¥50bn/ 100	Bank of China	3/86 - 4/96	5.30%/ NA	Nomura	NA	SAMURAI/PP	
	¥20bn/ 101.5	China Int'l Trust & Investment Corp	7/86 - 1/92	7.875%/ NA	Yamaichi Securities	NA	SAMURAI/PP	
	¥30bn/ 100	China Int'l Trust & Investment Corp	7/86 - 4/97	4.90%/ NA	Daiwa Securities	NA	SAMURAI/PP	
	¥40bn/ 99.7	China Int'l Trust & Investment Corp	9/86 - 2/96	6.30%/ NA	Daiwa Securities	NA	SAMURAI/PP	
	¥20bn/ 100	Guangdong Int'l Trust Investment	9/86 - 9/96	6.10%/ NA	Nomura	NA	SAMURAI/PP	
	¥20bn/ 101.5	China Int'l Trust & Investment Corp	12/86 - 1/92	7.875%/ NA	Yamaichi Securities	NA	SAMURAI/PP	
	¥10bn/ 101.875	China Int'l Trust & Investment Corp	2/87 - 2/92	2 yrs at 1.00% 3 yrs at 7.875%/ NA	Yamaichi International	NA	SAMURAI/PP	
	¥30bn/ 100	China Int'l Trust & Investment Corp	3/87 - 4/97	4.90%/ NA	Daiwa Securities	NA	SAMURAI/PP	
	¥20bn/ 100	Guangdong Int'l Trust Investment	3/87 - 9/96	6.10%/ NA	Nomura	NA	SAMURAI/PP	
	¥15bn/ 99.7	Bank of China	7/87 - 2/92	5.20%/ NA	Nikko	NA	SAMURAI/PP	
	¥10bn/ 99.75	Fujian Investment & Enterprise Corp	8/87 - 8/97	4.8%/ NA	Nomura	NA	SAMURAI/PP	
	¥15bn/ 102.625	China Int'l Trust & Investment Corp	12/87 - 12/93	5.625%/ NA	Nomura International	NA	SAMURAI/PP	
	¥15bn/ 101.875	Bank of China	1/88 - 1/93	5.00%/ NA	Yamaichi International	NA	SAMURAI/PP	
	¥20bn/ 101.875	Guangdong Int'l Trust Investment	3/88 - 3/93	5.125%/ NA	LTCB International	NA	SAMURAI/PP	
	¥15bn/ 101.625	Shanghai Ivestment & Trust Corp.	5/88 - 5/95	5.25%/ NA	Nomura International	NA	SAMURAI/PP	
	¥15bn/ 101.875	China Int'l Trust & Investment Corp	7/88 - 7/93	5.25%/ NA	Nikko Merchant Bank	NA	SAMURAI/PP	
	¥20bn/ 101.35	Bank of China	4/89 - 4/99	5.30%/ NA	Nomura	NA	SAMURAI/PP	
	¥25bn/ 100	Shangai Investment & Trust Corp.	10/89 - 2/96	6.60%/ NA	Nomura	NA	SAMURAI/PP	

COLOMBIA

DEBT TYPE	ISSUE SIZE/ PRICE	BORROWER	ISSUE DATE	COUPON/ LAUNCH YIELD	UNDERWRITER	SECURITY/ GUARANTEE	MARKET	COMMENTS
US$ FLOATING:	US$50m/ 100	Republic of Columbia	4/87 - 4/94	6M LIBOR+1.125%/ NA	Citicorp Investment Bank	NA	EURO	
	US$200m/ 100	Republic of Columbia	Two US$100m: 1/91 - 1/96 1/92 - 1/97 (two year grace)	LIBOR + 1.5%	Chemical Bank of London (agent)			•This deal was part of a refinancing agreement. The purchasers of the bonds were commercial creditors, though the instruments can then be sold and traded.
YEN:	¥6bn/ 100	Republic of Columbia	9/89 - 9/94	6.90%/ NA	IBJ	NA	SAMURAI/PP	

CZECHOSLOVAKIA

DEBT TYPE	ISSUE SIZE/ PRICE	BORROWER	ISSUE DATE	COUPON/ LAUNCH YIELD	UNDERWRITER	SECURITY/ GUARANTEE	MARKET	COMMENTS
DM:	DM250m/ 100.75	Ceskoslovenska Obchodni banka	7/90 - 8/95	10.00%/ NA	Commerzbank	Unsecured	EURO	
	DM350m/ 101	Ceskoslovenska Obchodni Banka	9/90 - 10/95	10.00%/ NA	Deutsche Bank	Unsecured	EURO	

DEBT TYPE	ISSUE SIZE/ PRICE	BORROWER	ISSUE DATE	COUPON/ LAUNCH YIELD	UNDERWRITER	SECURITY/ GUARANTEE	MARKET	COMMENTS
YEN:	¥10bn/ 100	Ceskoslovenska Obchodni Banka	11/86 - 5/99	5.70%/ NA	Nomura	NA	SAMURAI/PP	
	¥10bn/ 100	Ceskoslovenska Obchodni Banka	11/86 - 6/98	5.50%/ NA	Sumitomo	NA	SAMURAI/PP	

HUNGARY

DEBT TYPE	ISSUE SIZE/ PRICE	BORROWER	ISSUE DATE	COUPON/ LAUNCH YIELD	UNDERWRITER	SECURITY/ GUARANTEE	MARKET	COMMENTS
US$ FIXED:	US$200m/ 99.6	State Development Institute	8/90 - 8/00	10.50%/ NA	Daiwa Europe	Government Guarantee	EURO	•Principal guaranteed by IBRD
	US$100m/ 97.2	National Bank of Hungary	6/91 - 7/96	10.50%/ 11.26%	Bankers Trust	NA	EURO	
US$ FLOATING:	US$100m/ 100	National Bank of Hungary	1/86 - 1/01	Variable/ NA	Daiwa Singapore	Unsecured	EURO	
DM:	DM150m/ 100	National Bank of Hungary	2/86 - 2/96	7.25%/ NA	Dresdner Bank	NA	EURO	
	DM150m/ 100.38	National Bank of Hungary	9/86 - 9/96	6.875%/ NA	Westdeutsche Landesbank	NA	EURO	
	DM200m/ 100.25	National Bank of Hungary	3/87 - 3/94	6.75%/ NA	Dresdner Bank	NA	EURO	
	DM200m/ 100	National Bank of Hungary	3/88 - 3/95	6.25%/ NA	DG Bank	NA	EURO	
	DM200m/ 100.25	National Bank of Hungary	7/88 - 7/94	6.25%/ NA	Deutsche Bank	NA	EURO	
	DM200m/ 100	National Bank of Hungary	2/89 - 2/96	6.625%/ NA	Bayerische Vereinsbank Int'l	NA	EURO	
	DM200m/ 100	National Bank of Hungary	6/89 - 6/97	8.00%/ NA	DG Bank	NA	EURO	
	DM300m/ 100	National Bank of Hungary	2/90 - 2/97	10.00%/ NA	Commerzbank	NA	EURO	
	DM200m/ 100	National Bank of Hungary	5/90 - 5/96	9.75%/ NA	DG Bank Deutsche Genossenschaftsbank	NA	EURO	
	DM200m/ 100.25	National Bank of Hungary	10/90 - 10/95	10.00%/ NA	Deutsche Bank	NA	EURO	
	DM200m/ 99.75	National Bank of Hungary	3/91 - 3/96	10.50%/ 11.11%	Commerzbank	NA	EURO	
	DM150m/ NA	National Bank of Hungary	4/91 - 4/96	10.5%/ NA	Commerzbank	NA	EURO	
	DM200m/ NA	National Bank of Hungary	5/91 (paper maturities are variable)	Fixed, floating, and zero coupon	Deutsche Bank	NA	EURO	•Program is unrated and notes may be issued with call option
YEN:	¥40bn/ 99.65	National Bank of Hungary	9/87 - 10/97	6.30%/ NA	Daiwa Securities	NA	SAMURAI/PP	
	¥20bn/ 100	National Bank of Hungary	1/87 - 2/97	5.70%/ NA	Daiwa Securities	NA	SAMURAI/PP	
	¥25bn/ 99.75	National Bank of Hungary	3/88 - 3/98	5.70%/ NA	Daiwa Securities	NA	SAMURAI/PP	
	¥30bn/ 100.5	National Bank of Hungary	10/88 - 10/98	5.90%/ NA	Daiwa Securities	NA	SAMURAI/PP	
	¥10bn/ 100	National Bank of Hungary	2/89 - 3/96	6.40%/ NA	IBJ	NA	SAMURAI/PP	
	¥20bn/ 100	National Bank of Hungary	3/89 - 2/97	5.70%/ NA	Daiwa Securities	NA	SAMURAI/PP	
	¥25bn/ 100.5	National Bank of Hungary	3/89 - 9/99	6.00%/ NA	Daiwa Securities	NA	SAMURAI/PP	

DEBT TYPE	ISSUE SIZE/ PRICE	BORROWER	ISSUE DATE	COUPON/ LAUNCH YIELD	UNDERWRITER	SECURITY/ GUARANTEE	MARKET	COMMENTS
	¥25bn/ 99.75	National Bank of Hungary	3/89 - 3/98	5.70%/ NA	Daiwa Securities	NA	SAMURAI/PP	
	¥30bn/ 100.5	National Bank of Hungary	3/89 - 10/98	5.90%/ NA	Daiwa Securities	NA	SAMURAI/PP	
	¥35bn/ 100.9	National Bank of Hungary	3/89 - 3/99	5.70%/ NA	Daiwa Securities	NA	SAMURAI/PP	
	¥40bn/ 99.85	National Bank of Hungary	3/89 - 10/97	6.30%/ NA	Daiwa Securities	NA	SAMURAI/PP	
	¥25bn/ 100.5	National Bank of Hungary	9/89 - 9/99	6.00%/ NA	Daiwa Securities	NA	SAMURAI/PP	
SFR:	SFr50m/ 100	National Bank of Hungary	2/87 - 2/94	5.375%/ NA	Banque Gutzwiller Kurz Bungener	NA	EURO	
	SFr75m/ 100	National Bank of Hungary	11/88 - 11/94	5.50%/ NA	S G Warburg	NA	EURO	
OTHERS:	ECU75m/ 101.88	National Bank of Hungary	9/89 - 9/96	10.00%/ NA	Kredietbank SA Luxembourg	NA	EURO	
	ASch/1,500m NA	National Bank of Hungary	9/89 - 9/96	8.25%/ NA	Oesterreichische Laenderbank	NA	NA	
	ASch1000m/ 99.45	National Bank of Hungary	2/90 - 2/97	9.50%/ NA	Creditastalt- Bankverein	NA	EURO	
	ASch/500m 99	National Bank of Hungary	9/90 - 9/97	10.75%/ NA	Oesterreichische Laenderbank	NA	EURO	

INDIA

DEBT TYPE	ISSUE SIZE/ PRICE	BORROWER	ISSUE DATE	COUPON/ LAUNCH YIELD	UNDERWRITER	SECURITY/ GUARANTEE	MARKET	COMMENTS
US$ FIXED:	US$125m/ 101.65	Oil and Natural Gas Commission	12/88 - 11/93	9.75%/ NA	CSFB	Republic of India	EURO	
	US$100m/ NA	Industrial Dev Bank of India	6/89 - 6/96	10.00%/ NA	CSFB	Republic of India	EURO	
	US$125m/ 101.85	Oil and Natural Gas Commission	3/90 - 3/97	10.00%/ NA	CSFB	Republic of India	EURO	
US$ FLOATING:	US$200m/ 100	Indian Oil Corp.	11/89 - 11/94	Variable/ NA	CSFB	Republic of India	EURO	
DM:	DM100m/ 99.75	Industrial Dev Bank of India	2/86 - 2/93	7.00%/ NA	Dresdner Bank	Republic of India	EURO	
	DM150m/ 100	Oil and Natural Gas Commission	2/87 - 2/94	6.375%/ NA	Commerzbank	Republic of India	EURO	
	DM200m/ 100.5	Industrial Dev Bank of India	12/87 - 12/94	6.375%/ NA	Commerzbank	Republic of India	EURO	
	DM250m/ 100.25	Industrial Dev Bank of India	9/88 - 9/95	6.625%/ NA	Dresdner Bank	Republic of India	EURO	
	DM250m/ 100.625	Oil and Natural Gas Commission	6/90 - 6/97	9.50%/ NA	Commerzbank	Republic of India	EURO	
YEN:	¥20bn/ 101.35	Industrial Dev Bank of India	10/87 - 10/99	5.70%/ NA	Daiwa Securities	NA	SAMURAI/PP	
	¥5bn/ 100	Industrial Dev Bank of India	11/87 - 5/96	6.30%/ NA	Mitsui	NA	SAMURAI/PP	
	¥15bn/ 101.875	State Bank of India	5/88 - 5/93	5.25%/ NA	IBJ Int'l	NA	SAMURAI/PP	
	¥20bn/ 100.5	Oil and Natural Gas Commission	8/88 - 8/98	5.90%/ NA	Nomura	NA	SAMURAI/PP	
	¥20bn/ 101.2	Oil and Natural Gas Commission	3/89 - 3/99	5.50%/ NA	Nomura Securities	NA	SAMURAI/PP	

DEBT TYPE	ISSUE SIZE/ PRICE	BORROWER	ISSUE DATE	COUPON/ LAUNCH YIELD	UNDERWRITER	SECURITY/ GUARANTEE	MARKET	COMMENTS
	¥10bn/ 100	Oil and Natural Gas Commission	5/89 - 2/93	6.60%/ NA	Yasuda	NA	SAMURAI/PP	
	¥20bn/ 100.5	Oil and Natural Gas Commission	6/89 - 8/98	5.90%/ NA	Nomura	NA	SAMURAI/PP	
	¥20bn/ 101.2	Oil and Natural Gas Commission	6/89 - 4/99	5.50%/ NA	Nomura	NA	SAMURAI/PP	
	¥20bn/ 101.35	Industrial Dev Bank of India	9/89 - 10/99	5.70%/ NA	Daiwa Securities	NA	SAMURAI/PP	
SFR:	Up to SFr100m/ 100	Industrial Dev Bank of India	2/87 - 2/97	5.625%/ NA	Swiss Bank Corporation	Republic of India	EURO	
	SFr150m/ 100.125	Oil and Natural Gas Commission	3/88 - 3/98	5.375%/ NA	Credit Suisse	Republic of India	EURO	
	SFr80m/ 100.5	Industrial Credit and Investment Corp of India	7/88 - 7/95	5.25%/ NA	Swiss Bank Corporation	Republic of India	EURO	

INDONESIA

DEBT TYPE	ISSUE SIZE/ PRICE	BORROWER	ISSUE DATE	COUPON/ LAUNCH YIELD	UNDERWRITER	SECURITY/ GUARANTEE	MARKET	COMMENTS
US FIXED:	US$80m/ 100	Bank Expor Impor Indonesia	7/90 - 7/95	9.45%/ NA	Sumitomo	NA	EURO	
US$ FLOATING:	US$125m/ NA	Bank Expor Impor Indonesia	7/90 - NA	NA	JP Morgan	NA	NA	
	US$300m/ 100	Republic of Indonesia	2/86 - 2/01	Variable/ NA	Chase Manhattan	NA	EURO	
	US$135m/ NA	Bank Dagang Negara	Undated	Variable/ NA	JP Morgan	NA	NA	•For Bank Dagang's Cayman Island Branch
DM:	DM300m/ 100	Republic of Indonesia	10/88 - 10/93	6.375%/ NA	Commerzbank	NA	EURO	

KOREA

DEBT TYPE	ISSUE SIZE/ PRICE	BORROWER	ISSUE DATE	COUPON/ LAUNCH YIELD	UNDERWRITER	SECURITY/ GUARANTEE	MARKET	COMMENTS
US$ FIXED:	US$40m/ 100	Daewoo Corp.	5/86 - 12/01	3.00%/ NA	Nomura International	NA	EURO	•Convertible
	US$20m/ 100	Yukong	7/86 - 12/01	3.00%/ NA	Goldman Sachs International	NA	EURO	•Convertible
	US$30m/ 100	Goldstar	8/87 - 12/02	1.75%/ NA	Merrill Lynch Capital Markets	NA	EURO	
	US$50m/ 100.75	Samsung Semiconductor	7/88 - 7/95	9.875%/ NA	CSFB	Samsung Electronics	EURO	
	US$30m/ 100	Saehan Media Corporation	10/88 - 12/03	1.750%/ NA	Citicorp Scrimgeour Vickers Int'l	NA	EURO	•Convertible
	US$50m/ 100	Sammi Steel	11/89 - 11/94	1.250%/ NA	Merrill Lynch Int'l	NA	EURO	
	US$30m/ 100	STC Corp.	1/90 - 12/04	1.25%/ NA	CSFB	NA	EURO	•Convertible
	US$50m/ 100	Dong Ah Construction	2/90 - 12/04	1.25%/ NA	Swiss Bank Corp (London)	NA	EURO	•Convertible
	US$70m/ 100	Hyundai Motor	2/90 - 2/95	1.25%/ NA	CSFB	NA	EURO	
	US$30m/ 100	Samick Music	3/90 - 12/04	1.00%/ NA	Ssangyong Invs & Securities Co	NA	EURO	•Convertible

DEBT TYPE	ISSUE SIZE/ PRICE	BORROWER	ISSUE DATE	COUPON/ LAUNCH YIELD	UNDERWRITER	SECURITY/ GUARANTEE	MARKET	COMMENTS
	US$30m/ 100	Miwon	7/90 - 12/05	1.750%/ NA	Morgan Stanley International	NA	EURO	-Convertible
	US$300m/ NA	Korea Development Bank	12/90 - 12/00		Goldman Sachs	NA	YANKEE	
US$ FLOATING:	US$25m/ 100	Seangyong (USA) Inc.	1/87 - 1/92	6M LIBOR+0.25%/ NA	Bankers Trust International	Seangyong Corp & Cement	EURO	
	US$100m/ NA	Export Import Bank of Korea	3/87 - 3/90	LIBOR+0.125%/ NA	Bankers Trust Asia	NA	EURO	
	US$175m/ 100	Daewoo Corp.	7/87 - 7/95	LIBOR+0.1875%/ NA	LTCB International	NA	EURO	
	US$100m/ 100	Export Import Bank of Korea	8/87 - 8/90	Variable/ NA	Bankers Trust Asia Limited	NA	EURO	
	US$30m/ 100	Hyosung America	6/88 - 6/91	6M LIBOR+0.25%/ NA	Daiwa Securities	Hyosung Corp & Tongyang Nylon	EURO	
	US$30m/ 100	Yukong Ltd	12/88 - 12/96	5yrs at 0.10%L6 5yrs at 0.125%L6/ NA	Baring Brothers	NA	EURO	
	US$100m/ 100	Dong Ah Construction	1/90 - 1/00	Variable/ NA	Swiss Bank Corporation	NA	EURO	
	US$200m/ 100	Korea Development Bank	6/90 - 6/97	Variable/ NA	JP Morgan (Asia)	NA	EURO	
	US$100m/ NA	Export Import Bank of Korea	9/90 - 9/97	Variable/ NA	LTCB Asia Ltd	NA	NA	
	US$50m/ 100	Sunkyong Industries	3/91 - 4/98	3MLIBOR+0.375%/ NA	Manufacturers Hanover	NA	EURO	
	US$50m/ NA	Korea Intl. Merchant Bank	4/91 - 4/94	Variable/ NA	Commerzbank KEB International	NA	EURO	
DM:	DM100m/ 100	Export Import Bank of Korea	3/86 - 3/91	6.875%/ NA	DG Bank	NA	EURO	
	DM100m/ 99.75	Korea Development Bank	6/86 - 6/93	6.625%/ NA	Deutsche Bank	NA	EURO	
	DM 200m/ 101	Korea Development Bank	12/90 - 12/95	9.00%/ NA	Bayerische Landesbank Girozentrale	NA	EURO	
YEN:	¥30bn/ 99.7	Korea Exchange Bank	1/86 - 1/96	6.80%/ NA	Daiwa Securities	NA	SAMURAI/PP	
	¥20bn/ 100	Korea Electric Power Corporation	5/86 - 5/96	6.00%/ NA	Nikko	NA	SAMURAI/PP	
	¥7.5bn/ 101.375	Korea Electric Power Company	6/87 - 6/93	4.50%/ NA	Daiwa Europe	NA	SAMURAI/PP	
	¥30bn/ 101.2	Korea Development Bank	12/88 - 12/94	6.10%/ NA	Daiwa Securities	NA	SAMURAI/PP	
	¥20bn/ 100	Korea Electric Power Corporation	12/88 - 5/96	6.00%/ NA	Nikko	NA	SAMURAI/PP	
	¥30bn/ 99.7	Korea Exchange Bank	12/88 - 1/96	6.80%/ NA	Daiwa Securities	NA	SAMURAI/PP	
	¥30bn/ 101.2	Korea Development Bank	12/89 - 12/94	6.10%/ NA	Yamaichi Securities	NA	SAMURAI/PP	
OTHERS:	ECU105m/ 101.625	Export Import Bank of Korea	4/90 - 4/95	11.00%/ NA	Merrill Lynch	NA	EURO	

MALAYSIA

DEBT TYPE	ISSUE SIZE/ PRICE	BORROWER	ISSUE DATE	COUPON/ LAUNCH YIELD	UNDERWRITER	SECURITY/ GUARANTEE	MARKET	COMMENTS
US$ FIXED:	US$200m/ 101.38	Malaysia	10/89 - 10/96	9.50%/ NA	Goldman Sachs International	NA	EURO	

DEBT TYPE	ISSUE SIZE/ PRICE	BORROWER	ISSUE DATE	COUPON/ LAUNCH YIELD	UNDERWRITER	SECURITY/ GUARANTEE	MARKET	COMMENTS
	US$200m/ 99	Malaysia	10/90 - 10/00	9.875%/ 10.04%	Salomon Brothers	NA	YANKEE	
DM:	DM150m/ 100	Malaysia	6/87 - 6/94	6.25%/ NA	Deutsche Bank	NA	EURO	
	DM100m/ 100	Malaysia	4/88 - 4/95	6.00%/ NA	Deutsche Bank	NA	EURO	
YEN:	Y30bn/ 99.75	Government of Malaysia	2/88 - 2/98	5.60%/ NA	Nomura Securities	NA	SAMURAI/PP	
	Y30bn/ 101	Malaysia	12/88 - 3/99	5.40%/ NA	Daiwa Securities	NA	SAMURAI/PP	
	Y30bn/ 99.75	Malaysia	12/88 - 3/98	5.60%/ NA	Nomura	NA	SAMURAI/PP	
	Y30bn/ 101	Malaysia	3/89 - 3/99	5.40%/ NA	Daiwa Securities	NA	SAMURAI/PP	
SFR:	SFr125m/ 100.2	Malaysia	4/87 - 4/97	5.75%/ NA	Swiss Bank Corporation	NA	EURO	
	Sfr100m/ 100.25	Malaysia	6/88 - 6/98	5.25%/ NA	Credit Suisse	NA	EURO	

MEXICO

DEBT TYPE	ISSUE SIZE/ PRICE	BORROWER	ISSUE DATE	COUPON/ LAUNCH YIELD	UNDERWRITER	SECURITY/ GUARANTEE	MARKET	COMMENTS
US$ FIXED:	US$52m/ NA	Grupo Sanluis	10/88 - 10/90	NA/ 16.00%	Operadora da Bolsa	Grupo Sanluis	US Private Placement	-First private sector issue
	US$100m/ 88.45	Banco Nacional de Comercio Ext (BANCOMEXT)	6/89 - 6/94	10.25% 17.00%	Merrill Lynch	UMS	EURO	-First public sector offering since 1982 -Quarterly principal & interest
	US$150m/ 92.65	Cementos Mexicanos (CEMEX) Sunbelt	10/89 - 10/91	11.00%/ 16.00%	Citibank	CEMEX	EURO	-First major post 1982 issue -Callable 6 months/put 1 yr -Private sector
	US$65m/ 95.49	Empresas La Moderna (ELM Int'l)	1/90 - 7/92	13.50%/ 16.37%	Bear Stearns	Collateral pool of two companies	EURO	-97% Peso revenues -Private sector
	US$230m/ NA	Comision Federal de Electricidad	3/90 - 3/95	NA/ 11.50%	Salomon Brothers	Electricity receivables	US private placement	-Securitised issue
	US$900m/ NA (3 deals)	Telefonos de Mexico (TELMEX)	3/90 - 3/95	NA/ ca: 11.00%	Citibank	AT&T receivables	US private placement	-Securitised issue -Public sector
	US$33m/ 100	Tamtrade (Tamsa)	4/90 - 4/92	12.00%/ 13.00%	Bankers Trust International	Deposit with Bancomer (London)	EURO	-Private sector
	US$22m/ 92.65	Ponderossa	5/90 - 5/92	11.00%/ 16.00%	Lazards	NA	EURO	-Private sector
	US$130m/ NA	Banamex	6/90 - 6/93	NA/ ca: 9.50%	Citibank	Credit card receivables	US private placement	-Securitised
	US$100m/ NA	CEMEX Sunbelt Ent.	6/90 - 6/02	11.00%/13.50% 13.54% reset	Citibank	CEMEX	EURO	-Private sector
	US$100m	NAFINSA	7/90 - 8/95	11.75%/ 12.45%	First Boston	United Mexican States (UMS)	EURO	-Put option @ 3 years -Public sector
	US$150m/ NA	TELMEX	7/90 - 1/92	12.25%/ 13.00%	J.P. Morgan	Senior Unsecured	US private placement 144A	-Issuer takes withholding tax risk -Change of control put -Public sector
	US$100m/ 99.7	PEMEX	8/90 - 8/95	11.43%/ NA	Paine Webber	Unsecured	US private placement	-US domestic private placement with 6 insurance companies -Public sector
	US$65m/ NA	Novum	9/90 - 9/93	12%.00s.a./ 15.25%(to call)	1st Interstate	Novum is 90% owned by DESC	NA	-Call after year 2 -Private sector
	US$150m/ 99.7	PEMEX	9/90 - 9/93	11.625%/ NA	Swiss Bank Corporation	NA	NA	

DEBT TYPE	ISSUE SIZE/ PRICE	BORROWER	ISSUE DATE	COUPON/ LAUNCH YIELD	UNDERWRITER	SECURITY/ GUARANTEE	MARKET	COMMENTS
	US$75m/ NA	Sanluis (Barton Corp)	9/90 - 9/93	12.00%q/ 14.24%	Bankers Trust International	Collateralised by Time Deposit	EURO	•Issuer: Barton Corp. owned by Sanluis; 100% deposit with Banca Serfin (Loondon) •Public sector
	US$60m/ 95.75	Grupo Desc	9/90 - 9/93	12.00%/ NA	Banco Santander First Interstate Bancomer	NA	NA	
	US$70m/ 93.73	Banca Serfin	1/91 - 1/96	10.50%/ NA	Yamaichi	NA	NA	
	US$ 125m/ 99.4	PEMEX	2/91 - 2/93	10.00%/ NA	Swiss Bank Corporation	Unsecured	EURO	•State Oil Company
	US$ 125m/ 100	NAFINSA	4/91 - 5/96	10.00%/ 10.00%	JP Morgan	NA	EURO	•Put option at par 14-May-93
	US$425 m/ 99.75	CEMEX	5/91 - 5/96	9.41%/ 15.03%	JP Morgan	Unsecured	One tranche is EURO the other is 144a	
	US$50m/ 100	TAMSA	6/91 - 6/97	7.5%/ NA	Bankers Trust	NA	EURO	
	US$100m/ 100	BANCOMEXT	6/91- 6/96	9.875%/ 9.64%	NA	NA	EURO	
	US$100m/ 100.55	Banobras	8/91 - 8/96	10.75%/ NA	Credit Suisse First Boston	NA	EURO	
US$ FLOATING:	US$30m/ NA	Transportacion Maratima Mexicana	6/89 - 6/96	LIBOR + 1.5%	Citibank	NA	US private placement	
	US$230m/ NA	Bancomer	7/90 - 7/95	LIBOR + 5/8%/ NA	Citibank	Credit card receivables	US private placement	•Securitised
	US$570m/ NA	TELMEX	1/91-1/96	US T bills + 1.50%	Citibank	Long Distance Receivables	US private placement	•Securitised
DM:	DM100m/ NA	PEMEX	4/90 - 4/95	11.25%/ 11.80%	West LB	PEMEX	EURO	•first DM Eurobond by Mexican borrower since 1982
	DM150m/ NA	NAFINSA	6/90 - 5/95	11.00%/ 11.55%	Dresdner	UMS	EURO	•Public Sector
	DM100m/ NA	BANCOMEXT	7/90 - 7/95	11.00%/ 11.55%	SBC	UMS	EURO	•Public Sector
	DM300m/ 100.5	United Mexican States	2/91 - 3/96	10.50%/ 10.37%	Deutsche Bank	NA	EURO	
OTHERS:	ASch500m/ NA	PEMEX	7/90 - 7/96	11.00%/ 11.47%	Credit - Anstalt	PEMEX	EURO	•Strong retail & inst. demand •First Austrian Schilling issue
	ECU100m/ 100.05	PEMEX	8/90 - 8/94	11.50%/ 11.17%	NA	PEMEX	EURO	

NAURU, REPUBLIC OF

DEBT TYPE	ISSUE SIZE/ PRICE	BORROWER	ISSUE DATE	COUPON/ LAUNCH YIELD	UNDERWRITER	SECURITY/ GUARANTEE	MARKET	COMMENTS
YEN:	Y4bn/ 100	Republic of Nauru Finance Co Ltd	10/89 - 5/95	6.50%/ NA	Yamaichi Securities	NA	SAMURAI/PP	
	Y4bn/ 99.5	Republic of Nauru Finance Co Ltd	10/89 - 1/93	7.50%/ NA	Daiwa Securities	NA	SAMURAI/PP	
	Y5bn/ 100	Republic of Nauru Finance Co Ltd	10/89 - 7/94	7.00%/ NA	Daiwa Securities	NA	SAMURAI/PP	

PANAMA

DEBT TYPE	ISSUE SIZE/ PRICE	BORROWER	ISSUE DATE	COUPON/ LAUNCH YIELD	UNDERWRITER	SECURITY/ GUARANTEE	MARKET	COMMENTS
US$ FLOATING:	US$30m/ NA	Republic of Panama	3/87 - 3/92	LIBOR + 1.75%/ NA	IBJ	NA	NA	

DEBT TYPE	ISSUE SIZE/ PRICE	BORROWER	ISSUE DATE	COUPON/ LAUNCH YIELD	UNDERWRITER	SECURITY/ GUARANTEE	MARKET	COMMENTS
SINGAPORE								
US$FIXED:	US$75m/ 100	Keppel Corp	9/87 - 9/97	2.75% - 3.00%	Morgan Grenfell	NA	EURO	-Convertible
	US$75m/ 100	DBS Land	2/90 - 2/95	1.00%/ NA	Daiwa Europe	NA	EURO	
	US$75m/ 100	DBS Land	3/90 - 3/95	1.00%/ NA	Daiwa Europe	NA	EURO	
	US$75m/ 100	DBS Land	3/90 - 3/95	1.00%/ NA	Daiwa Europe	NA	EURO	
US$ FLOATING:	US$50m/ 100	Export Credit Insurance Corp.	1/87 - 1/92	Variable/ NA	Standard Chartered Mercahnt Bank (Asia)	NA	EURO	
OTHERS:	S$20m/ 100	Jurong Town Corp	8/87 - 8/88	4.00%/ NA	SIMBL	NA	EURO	
	S$20m/ 100	Jurong Town Corp	8/87 - 8/89	4.0625%/ NA	SIMBL	NA	EURO	
	S$20m/ 100	Jurong Town Corp	8/87 - 8/90	4.75%/ NA	SIMBL	NA	EURO	
	S$20m/ 100	Jurong Town Corp	8/87 - 8/91	5.50%/ NA	SIMBL	NA	EURO	
	S$20m/ 100	Jurong Town Corp	8/87 - 8/92	5.75%/ NA	SIMBL	NA	EURO	
	ECU75m/ 100	Keppel Corp.	4/87 - 7/97	4.00%/ NA	Morgan Grenfell	NA	EURO	-Convertible
TAIWAN								
US$ FIXED:	US$100m/ 100	Yuen Foong Yu Paper	12/89 - 12/99	2.00%/ NA	Bankers Trust International	NA	EURO	
THAILAND								
US$ FIXED:	US$200m/ 100	Kingdom of Thailand	7/89 - 8/99	8.70%/ NA	Salomon Brothers	NA	YANKEE	
DM:	DM200m/ 100.125	Kingdom of Thailand	7/88 - 7/93	5.75%/ NA	Commerzbank	NA	EURO	
SFR:	SwFr200m/ 99.75	Kingdom of Thailand	6/88 - 6/95	4.625%/ NA	Credit Suisse	NA	EURO	
TRINIDAD & TOBAGO								
YEN:	¥7.5bn/ 100	Trinidad & Tobago	2/87 - 2/94	6.80%/ NA	Nikko Securities	NA	SAMURAI/PP	
	¥10bn/ 100	Trinidad & Tobago	3/88 - 3/93	6.50%/ NA	Nomura Securities	NA	SAMURAI/PP	
	¥7.5bn/ 100	Trinidad & Tobago	10/89 - 12/94	6.70%/ NA	Yamaichi Securitites	NA	SAMURAI/PP	
	¥7.5bn/ 100	Trinidad & Tobago	10/89 - 3/94	6.80%/ NA	Nikko	NA	SAMURAI/PP	
	¥10bn/ 100	Trinidad & Tobago	10/89 - 2/93	6.50%/ NA	Nomura	NA	SAMURAI/PP	

DEBT TYPE	ISSUE SIZE/ PRICE	BORROWER	ISSUE DATE	COUPON/ LAUNCH YIELD	UNDERWRITER	SECURITY/ GUARANTEE	MARKET	COMMENTS
TUNISIA								
US$ FIXED:	US$171m/ 100	Republic of Tunisia	9/88 - 9/94	9.125%/ NA	Citicorp Investment Bank	NA	Priavte Placement	
	US$25m/ 100	Republic of Tunisia	9/88 - 9/94	9.125%/ NA	Citicorp Investment Bank	NA	Priavte Placement	
TURKEY								
US$ FIXED:	US$150m/ 100	Republic of Turkey	12/88 - 12/98	11.125%/ NA	Bankers Trust International	NA	EURO	
	US$200m/ 100.25	Republic of Turkey	4/89 - 4/99	11.50%/ NA	JP Morgan Securities	NA	EURO	
	US$200m/ 100	Republic of Turkey	9/89 - 9/99	10.25%a/ NA	JP Morgan Securities	NA	EURO	
	US$250m/ 100	Republic of Turkey	11/89 - 11/95	9.75%a/ NA	Sumitomo International	NA	EURO	
	US$100m/ 100	Development Bank of Turkey	12/89 - 12/95	9.75%/ NA	Daiwa Europe	NA	EURO	
	US$200m/ 100.2	Republic of Turkey	3/90 - 3/97	10.75%/ NA	Mitsui Taiyo Kobe Finance Int'l	NA	EURO	
	US$150m/ 101.2	Republic of Turkey	8/90 - 8/95	10.375%/ NA	Daiwa Europe	NA	EURO	
DM:	DM125/ 100	Central Bank of Turkey	3/87 - 3/92	6.875%/ NA	Commerzbank AG	Republic of Turkey	EURO	
	DM200/ 100	Central Bank of Turkey	10/87 - 10/92	7.00%/ NA	Commerzbank AG	Republic of Turkey	EURO	
	DM200m/ 100	EXIM Bank Turkey	2/88 - 2/94	6.75%/ NA	Dresdner Bank AG	Republic of Turkey	EURO	
	DM300m/ 100	Central Bank of Turkey	3/88 - 3/95	6.75%/ NA	Commerzbank AG	Republic of Turkey	EURO	
	DM500m/ 100	Republic of Turkey	5/88 - 5/95	6.50%/ NA	Commerzbank AG	NA	EURO	
	DM300m/ 100	Republic of Turkey	11/88 - 11/95	6.50%/ NA	Dresdner Bank AG	NA	EURO	
	DM30m/ 100	Ram dis Ticaret	4/89 - 4/93	8.50%/ NA	JP Morgan GmbH	Koc Holdings	EURO	
	DM400m/ 100	Republic of Turkey	7/89 - 7/96	7.75%/ NA	Commerzbank AG	NA	EURO	
	DM250m/ 102	Republic of Turkey	4/90 - 4/97	10.00%/ NA	Commerzbank AG	NA	EURO	
	DM 150m/ 100	Greater Ankara Municipality	10/90 - 10/95	10.25%/ NA	DG Bank	Republic of Turkey	EURO	
	DM 350m/ 100.5	Republic of Turkey	5/91 - 5/96	10.50%/ NA	Commerzbank AG	NA	EURO	
YEN:	¥10bn/ 100	Central Bank of Turkey	6/86 - 11/96	6.30%/ NA	Yamaichi Securities	NA	SAMURAI/PP	
	¥10bn/ 100	Delvet Yatirim Bankasi	10/86 - 11/93	6.80%/ NA	Yasuda	NA	SAMURAI/PP	
	¥10bn/ 100	Development Bank of Turkey	12/86 - 6/99	6.10%/ NA	Daiwa Securities	NA	SAMURAI/PP	
	¥10bn/ 100	Export Credit Bank of Turkey	2/87 - 6/96	6.30%/ NA	Yamaichi Securities	NA	SAMURAI/PP	

DEBT TYPE	ISSUE SIZE/ PRICE	BORROWER	ISSUE DATE	COUPON/ LAUNCH YIELD	UNDERWRITER	SECURITY/ GUARANTEE	MARKET	COMMENTS
	¥9.5bn/ 100	Industrial Dev Bank of Turkey	2/87 - 2/94	6.70%/ NA	Nikko Securities Mitsui Bank	Republic of Turkey	SAMURAI/PP	
	¥9.5bn/ 100	Industrial Dev Bank of Turkey	11/87 - 2/94	6.70%/ NA	Nikko	NA	SAMURAI/PP	
	¥10bn/ 100	Industrial Dev Bank of Turkey	11/87 - 3/97	6.00%/ NA	Nikko	NA	SAMURAI/PP	
	¥10bn/ 100	TC Turizm Bankasi AS	3/88 - 3/95	6.40%/ NA	Nikko Securities	Republic of Turkey	SAMURAI/PP	
	¥10bn/ 100	Industrial Dev Bank of Turkey	2/89 - 2/97	6.00%/ NA	Nikko Securities	NA	SAMURAI/PP	

URUGUAY

DEBT TYPE	ISSUE SIZE/ PRICE	BORROWER	ISSUE DATE	COUPON/ LAUNCH YIELD	UNDERWRITER	SECURITY/ GUARANTEE	MARKET	COMMENTS
YEN:	¥3.75bn/ NA	Republic of Uruguay	11/90 - 11/95	6.70%/ NA	Nikko	NA	Private Placement	

VENEZUELA

DEBT TYPE	ISSUE SIZE/ PRICE	BORROWER	ISSUE DATE	COUPON/ LAUNCH YIELD	UNDERWRITER	SECURITY/ GUARANTEE	MARKET	COMMENTS
US$ FIXED:	US$100m/ 100	Republic of Venezuela	2/88 - 2/93	11.125%s/ NA	JP Morgan Securities	NA	EURO	
	US$35m/ 90.35	Corporacion Industrial Montana (CORIMON)	10/90 - 10/95	10.25%/ NA	Merrill Lynch	Corimon	EURO	•Interest Payable on quarterly basis •Principal paid in 16 Installments starting Jan 15, 1992 and ending Oct 15, 1995.
US$ FLOATING:	US$100m/ 100	Republic of Venezuela	8/88 - 8/93	LIBOR + 1 7/8%/ NA	Samuel Montagu	NA	EURO	
	US$166m/ 100	Republic of Venezuela	12/88 - 12/94	LIBOR + 1.125%/ NA	Banca Mercantil/ Chase	NA	EURO	
	US$167m/ 100	Republic of Venezuela	12/88 - 12/98	LIBOR + 1.125%/ NA	Banca Mercantil/ Chase	NA	EURO	
	US$167m/ 100	Republic of Venezuela	12/88 - 12/03	LIBOR + 1.125%/ NA	Banca Mercantil/ Chase	NA	EURO	
	US$263m/ 100	Republic of Venezuela	1/89 - 12/95	LIBOR + 1.25%/ NA	Samuel Montagu	NA	EURO	
	US$40m/ 84.38	Sivensa Steel	4/90 - 4/95	Variable/ NA	CSFB	NA	EURO	
	US$60m/ NA	Tytan Securities (Investment vehicle for SIDETUR)	12/90 - 5/96	LIBOR + 1.375%/ NA	Citibank	SIDETUR's receivables from Thyssen Sudamerica	EURO	•SIDETUR is a Venezuelan steel company to receive the $60m while it pays cash receivables (from a steel contract with Thyssen) to Tytan securities.
DM:	DM100m/ 100	Republic of Venezuela	11/88 - 11/93	8.25%/ NA	Westdeutsche Landesbank	NA	EURO	
	DM200m/ 100	Petroleos de Venezuela	9/90 - 10/95	11.125%/ 11.68% (less fees)	Bankers Trust GmbH	NA	EURO	•Petroleos de Venezuela's net profit in 1990 was $2.12 billion

Distributors of World Bank Publications

ARGENTINA
Carlos Hirsch, SRL
Galería Guemes
Florida 165, 4th Floor-Ofc. 453/465
1333 Buenos Aires

**AUSTRALIA, PAPUA NEW GUINEA,
FIJI, SOLOMON ISLANDS,
VANUATU, AND WESTERN SAMOA**
D.A. Books & Journals
648 Whitehorse Road
Mitcham 3132
Victoria

AUSTRIA
Gerold and Co.
Graben 31
A-1011 Wien

BAHRAIN
Bahrain Research and Consultancy
Associates Ltd.
P.O. Box 22103
Manama Town 317

BANGLADESH
Micro Industries Development
Assistance Society (MIDAS)
House 5, Road 16
Dhanmondi R/Area
Dhaka 1209

Branch offices:
Main Road
Maijdee Court
Noakhali - 3800

76, K.D.A. Avenue
Kulna

BELGIUM
Jean De Lannoy
Av. du Roi 202
1060 Brussels

CANADA
Le Diffuseur
C.P. 85, 1501 B rue Ampère
Boucherville, Québec
J4B 5E6

CHINA
China Financial & Economic
Publishing House
8, Da Fo Si Dong Jie
Beijing

COLOMBIA
Infoenlace Ltda.
Apartado Aereo 34270
Bogota D.E.

COTE D'IVOIRE
Centre d'Edition et de Diffusion
Africaines (CEDA)
04 B.P. 541
Abidjan 04 Plateau

CYPRUS
MEMRB Information Services
P.O. Box 2098
Nicosia

DENMARK
SamfundsLitteratur
Rosenoerns Allé 11
DK-1970 Frederiksberg C

DOMINICAN REPUBLIC
Editors Taller, C. por A.
Restauración e Isabel la Católica 309
Apartado Postal 2190
Santo Domingo

EL SALVADOR
Fusades
Avenida Manuel Enrique Araujo #3530
Edificio SISA, 1er. Piso
San Salvador

EGYPT, ARAB REPUBLIC OF
Al Ahram
Al Galaa Street
Cairo

The Middle East Observer
41, Sherif Street
Cairo

FINLAND
Akateeminen Kirjakauppa
P.O. Box 128
SF-00101
Helsinki 10

FRANCE
World Bank Publications
66, avenue d'Iéna
75116 Paris

GERMANY
UNO-Verlag
Poppelsdorfer Allee 55
D-5300 Bonn 1

GREECE
KEME
24, Ippodamou Street Platia Plastiras
Athens-11635

GUATEMALA
Librerías Piedra Santa
5a. Calle 7-55
Zona 1
Guatemala City

HONG KONG, MACAO
Asia 2000 Ltd.
46-48 Wyndham Street
Winning Centre
2nd Floor
Central Hong Kong

INDIA
Allied Publishers Private Ltd.
751 Mount Road
Madras - 600 002

Branch offices:
15 J.N. Heredia Marg
Ballard Estate
Bombay - 400 038

13/14 Asaf Ali Road
New Delhi - 110 002

17 Chittaranjan Avenue
Calcutta - 700 072

Jayadeva Hostel Building
5th Main Road Gandhinagar
Bangalore - 560 009

3-5-1129 Kachiguda Cross Road
Hyderabad - 500 027

Prarthana Flats, 2nd Floor
Near Thakore Baug, Navrangpura
Ahmedabad - 380 009

Patiala House
16-A Ashok Marg
Lucknow - 226 001

INDONESIA
Pt Indira Limited
Jl. Sam Ratulangi 37
P.O. Box 181
Jakarta Pusat

ITALY
Licosa Commissionaria Sansoni SPA
Via Benedetto Fortini, 120/10
Casella Postale 552
50125 Florence

JAPAN
Eastern Book Service
37-3, Hongo 3-Chome, Bunkyo-ku 113
Tokyo

KENYA
Africa Book Service (E.A.) Ltd.
P.O. Box 45245
Nairobi

KOREA, REPUBLIC OF
Pan Korea Book Corporation
P.O. Box 101, Kwangwhamun
Seoul

KUWAIT
MEMRB Information Services
P.O. Box 5465

MALAYSIA
University of Malaya Cooperative
Bookshop, Limited
P.O. Box 1127, Jalan Pantai Baru
Kuala Lumpur

MEXICO
INFOTEC
Apartado Postal 22-860
14060 Tlalpan, Mexico D.F.

MOROCCO
Société d'Etudes Marketing Marocaine
12 rue Mozart, Bd. d'Anfa
Casablanca

NETHERLANDS
InOr-Publikaties b.v.
P.O. Box 14
7240 BA Lochem

NEW ZEALAND
Hills Library and Information Service
Private Bag
New Market
Auckland

NIGERIA
University Press Limited
Three Crowns Building Jericho
Private Mail Bag 5095
Ibadan

NORWAY
Narvesen Information Center
Book Department
P.O. Box 6125 Etterstad
N-0602 Oslo 6

OMAN
MEMRB Information Services
P.O. Box 1613, Seeb Airport
Muscat

PAKISTAN
Mirza Book Agency
65, Shahrah-e-Quaid-e-Azam
P.O. Box No. 729
Lahore 3

PERU
Editorial Desarrollo SA
Apartado 3824
Lima

PHILIPPINES
International Book Center
Fifth Floor, Filipinas Life Building
Ayala Avenue, Makati
Metro Manila

POLAND
ORPAN
Palac Kultury i Nauki
00-901 Warszawa

PORTUGAL
Livraria Portugal
Rua Do Carmo 70-74
1200 Lisbon

SAUDI ARABIA, QATAR
Jarir Book Store
P.O. Box 3196
Riyadh 11471

MEMRB Information Services
Branch offices:
Al Alsa Street
Al Dahna Center
First Floor
P.O. Box 7188
Riyadh

Haji Abdullah Alireza Building
King Khaled Street
P.O. Box 3969
Damman

33, Mohammed Hassan Awad Street
P.O. Box 5978
Jeddah

**SINGAPORE, TAIWAN,
MYANMAR, BRUNEI**
Information Publications
Private, Ltd.
02-06 1st Fl., Pei-Fu Industrial
Bldg.
24 New Industrial Road
Singapore 1953

SOUTH AFRICA, BOTSWANA
For single titles:
Oxford University Press
Southern Africa
P.O. Box 1141
Cape Town 8000

For subscription orders:
International Subscription Service
P.O. Box 41095
Craighall
Johannesburg 2024

SPAIN
Mundi-Prensa Libros, S.A.
Castello 37
28001 Madrid

Librería Internacional AEDOS
Consell de Cent, 391
08009 Barcelona

SRI LANKA AND THE MALDIVES
Lake House Bookshop
P.O. Box 244
100, Sir Chittampalam A.
Gardiner Mawatha
Colombo 2

SWEDEN
For single titles:
Fritzes Fackboksforetaget
Regeringsgatan 12, Box 16356
S-103 27 Stockholm

For subscription orders:
Wennergren-Williams AB
Box 30004
S-104 25 Stockholm

SWITZERLAND
For single titles:
Librairie Payot
6, rue Grenus
Case postale 381
CH 1211 Geneva 11

For subscription orders:
Librairie Payot
Service des Abonnements
Case postale 3312
CH 1002 Lausanne

TANZANIA
Oxford University Press
P.O. Box 5299
Dar es Salaam

THAILAND
Central Department Store
306 Silom Road
Bangkok

**TRINIDAD & TOBAGO, ANTIGUA
BARBUDA, BARBADOS,
DOMINICA, GRENADA, GUYANA,
JAMAICA, MONTSERRAT, ST.
KITTS & NEVIS, ST. LUCIA,
ST. VINCENT & GRENADINES**
Systematics Studies Unit
#9 Watts Street
Curepe
Trinidad, West Indies

UNITED ARAB EMIRATES
MEMRB Gulf Co.
P.O. Box 6097
Sharjah

UNITED KINGDOM
Microinfo Ltd.
P.O. Box 3
Alton, Hampshire GU34 2PG
England

VENEZUELA
Librería del Este
Aptdo. 60.337
Caracas 1060-A

YUGOSLAVIA
Jugoslovenska Knjiga
P.O. Box 36
Trg Republike
YU-11000 Belgrade